Kant in Hong Kong

Kant in Hong Kong
Walking, Thinking, and the City

Published by EYECORNER PRESS
February 2014
Roskilde

ISBN: 978-87-92633-26-2

Cover design and layout:
Camelia Elias

Printed in the US and UK

Kant in Hong Kong

Walking, Thinking, and the City

by

GRAY KOCHHAR-LINDGREN

EYECORNER PRESS

For the partners in Blissful Dragon Enterprises: David Campion, Joseph Chaney, Po Chung, Janel Curry, Hedley Freake, Paul Hanstedt, Tom Osgood, David Pong, and Glenn Shive. And for my University of Hong Kong students in *Kant's Critical Philosophy*, who struggled alongside me with those texts that "smell of cruelty" and taste of pure delight.

Only thoughts reached by walking have value.

– Nietzsche, *Twilight of the Idols*

Reaching for his stained coveralls, he awakens in the half-light. He sips his morning tea as he watches from his window as the sun rises red then golden then white as it passes from the depths of the earth, from the depths of space, and appears slowly through the diaphanous morning mist. It languorously climbs the walls of the dilapidated public housing with the still moist laundry hanging from the balconies, up the walls of the posh apartments on Robinson Rd, and up the glittering polished glass of the multinational banks in Central before spreading over the hazy mountains in the distance. Placing his cup in the sink, the man steps out of the battered old door, takes the squeaking elevator to the ground floor, retrieves his mop and its metal bucket from the closet, and heads out for the park at the edge of Kennedy Town.

Attentively watching the men and women beginning their morning Tai Chi on the worn grass, he arcs his face to feel the warmth of the sun and the slightest of breezes drifting in from Victoria Harbor. His hands feel the worn wooden handle as he dips the mop into the bucket he has filled with water from the park's faucet and then he begins to work. In a slow improvised dance, his mop paints a character on the pavement. As the Tai Chi session ends, so, too, the writing slows to a halt. The man examines his work. Already the water, glistening in the morning light, is evaporating in the quickly increasing heat.

The calligraphy is vanishing as the man turns toward the day ahead, regretting that his skill has advanced so little over the lathed turning of the years. He will, tomorrow, practice once again. Now, though, he must mop the floors and clean the windows until, shining, they are carry the sun and the sea in their brightly illuminated surfaces.

§

25 Sha Wan Drive. In the morning darkness the lights on the off-loaders, the massive container ships, and the small quick scows rimmed with treadless tires reflect off the silken black waters of the Soi Pok Liu Hoi Hop, the Lamma Channel that serves as an off-ramp from the South China Sea into the anchorages of Victoria Harbor. From my green, lumpy, and ill-proportioned chair, I happily gaze out at the passing boats and the changing weather of late August, hot and hazy with a humidity that hits me like a big-rig of solid heat. We have just arrived in Hong Kong.

A ferry slides by, leaving a bright phosphorescence in its wake. Now it has passed from my sight, framed by the window and the balcony, though still it is presumably in the world. Why do we assume this? Because we assume, most of the time, that our individual perception does not constitute reality and that objects we perceive in the medio-scale of perception have an objective being that insures lastingness, for some period of time, beyond when they leave our sight. We also assume this of the world itself, that, as world, it subsists before and after our fleeting passage through what is called "life." The light is emanating from everywhere as it spreads itself evenly toward the expansion of the day. There is not a sharp demarcation line between sea, sky, and mountains, but only a gray surface tinted with the slightest hint of blue. The blue flushes with its own deepening.

Immanuel Kant, whom Nietzsche famously named the "Chinaman of Königsberg," is a great traveler, an adventurer of the high seas, even though he never left the flat plains of Prussia. He knows something of islands, reefs, riptides, and storms. He knows not a word of Chinese, however, and neither the bankers in Central, the villagers fishing along these coasts, or most of the professors ensconced in the city's halls of higher learning, know anything of the labyrinthine prose that Kant is writing or of the regularity of his daily walk that served Königsberg as a clock. Right, left; right, left. Walking in time; walking as time-keeping. All time depends on motion, but motion depends on time. Time for Kant does not, finally, depend on empirical motion such as the wheeling of the planets or the hurried orbit of the lunar sphere, but is, instead, an *a priori* form, which, along with space, gives us the transcendental aesthetic conditions for the possibility of any experience. Any experience at all. Copernicus has been transfigured by, and into, a philosopher.

The flat on Sha Wan Drive is extraordinarily spacious for the two of us, especially given the tiny subdivided boxes in which most Hong Kongers live. The wooden floor is a parquet pattern with strips of wood set perpendicularly against each other. The balcony entrance, with its sliding door and glass partitions, is divided into six sections that bisect and frame the view of the Lamma Channel. The balcony floor consists of small brown square tiles, 16 x 40, itself bordered by tiny blue tiles and protected by a black iron railing divided by a series of vertical supports. The world is a geometry of squares, rectangles; Descartes has been materialized as the architecture of the city. The world is number, but what is number? How does a simple arithmetic transaction occur? The heat is almost unbearable. How does Kant survive in his sturdy German waistcoat and breeches? In that baroque dusted wig? How, in fact, did Kant arrive here in Hong Kong at all?

Outside the humidity thickens, even this early in the morning. The great philosopher of critique is far from home, far from the flatlands, far from the heartland of Europe. What is he thinking about? What is "home" and what is "far from"? How could he even begin to think architectonically in this humidity? The Germans, perhaps, turn to philosophy, or to the Mediterranean, to make it through the ice of winter. What happens, though, when philosophy moves toward the tropics? What tropes start turning?

The flat boasts two bedrooms, a large living area, a kitchen with all the appliances of modernity, two bathrooms, and the servant's quarters in the back. That's what the tiny room in the back off the kitchen is called, apparently, a ghost of both the old colonialism and of contemporary capitalism, including the new State capitalist experiment regulated by Beijing. The empty tiled and concrete cubicle has its own toilet and sink, but only with a cold water outlet. That, surely, would be sufficient for the servant, for servants, apparently, do not need the luxury of hot water.

Water drips from the back of the air-conditioner, the power for which comes from the huge plant on Lamma Island, one of the "outlying" islands that is a short ferry ride from the Central Pier or from Aberdeen and whose stacks are just visible on a very clear day (of which there are few). A small drain is set in yet another square of tiles for the run-off. The tile and grout dealers must do a booming business. Below is the expanse of the university's recreation complex with the shimmering blue pool, the gym, and the lined cricket, baseball, and football fields, with the sea just on the other side of a barrier of rock. Hong Kong is a place of global collisions and collusions and all the sports of the world gamble with cash and credit in the Jockey Club, at Happy Valley, in the Mah Jong parlors and British bridge clubs, on the golf courses, and in the high dust-moted aeries of the powerhouses of international finance.

Culverts and drains are everywhere along Sha Wan Drive and throughout the city, for all of Hong Kong in built in a bowl or on the side of a mountain. Summer rains and typhoons blow through on a regular basis, triggering a Black Typhoon Warning or a #8 Rain Warning. Classes at the university are cancelled under such conditions, though if the students are in the middle of an exam, they must finish it. That is as it should be, since at any cost one must complete an exam in progress and guard with diligence against the human tendency to cheat. Kant would no doubt approve, already musing obliquely on the categorical imperative: if your action is universalizable, it is the right thing to do. Duty, emptied of interest, should overcome the anxiety occasioned by the contingent approach of a mere typhoon, though we will have to inquire more into the relationship between the storms of the sublime and the maxims of morality.

When I look out and down over my balcony at the strip of ground that lies between Tam Towers and the Channel, it is quite hazy at the moment with several ships moored in the near and middle distance as if they are emerging magically out of the haze, this all-encompassing background from which the world appears. Westminster Abbey emerging from the fog on the Thames, with the daubs of color-constellations indicating movement, the slow dynamism of fog, its patchiness, its tendrils, the way it conceals and reveals what is before us. Kant stepping out into the cold from his stolid door with the heavy lion-headed knocker that he so loves the solid sound of. It is somber and serious, like thought itself.

§

The Stanley Ho Swimming Pool is a gorgeous blue. The world brightens and the ferry churning in from Lamma comes into view, the mountains of Lantau appear as if from nowhere. The sun is burning through the clouds and the rugged mountains show-forth. Kant nods, quill in hand, as he sits nearby in his spectral form and peers out into the haze. I can't tell if he's sleeping or thinking, but how close the two are to each other in the dream, the meditation, the reflection.

The fresh morning sunlight shimmers off of the intense blueness of the swimming pool tucked away at the edge of the Channel inside the Stanley Ho Sports Complex. Sports from around the world converge in competition, that most wholesome act of training for capitalism. But it's the pool that is the lure for the imagination, for it is closest to our primordiality, our fundamentally amphibian and amphibolous essence. We come from water. Our bodies slosh about the streets as temporary water-carriers and bearers of an alien biome that buzzes around us as we walk, sleep, eat. Thales, the great Ionian philosopher, said "everything is water," for water is that element which is always changing form while, paradoxically, remaining the same. This is, in part, the question of time and of space.

What is it that forms the whole? That is, finally, a philosophical rather than a scientific question, for the "whole" can never be given in experience and therefore cannot be calculated or encapsulated by any possible set of observations. The mind always exceeds what is before-us, though the mind is flexible and can step back, turn on itself and out toward the cosmos. Kant will speak at length about infinity and its implications for knowledge, for which he makes strong but modest claims. David Hume is always the nightmare that disturbs his dream of reason, driving him ever more deeply into thinking that will establish the Copernican Revolution that accounts for the trustworthy causality of law that governs the motion of the planets, and, along the axis of freedom, for the moral law that grounds the principles of practical reason. In the end, the practical will exceed the speculative in value, for without freedom there can be nothing called science or knowledge.

The water in the pool is barely ruffled. The sea is just beyond the wall, the wide paved path, a narrow band of vegetation, and the beige rocks of the coastline. I have no idea what any of the trees or flowers are called, here in the subtropics with its multifarious blues and greens. I wish I had the eye of Van Gogh or Paul Klee. I wish I knew a local painter who experiences color on the skin of her eyes and on the peacock eyes of her skin.

Container ships from around the world are moored out in the bay, surrounded by crane-boats that shuttle around to transfer the ribbed steel boxes from the larger ships to smaller ones and then onto trucks and trains that head upriver to the Pearl River Delta and Guangdong, the "factory of the world" that is undergoing extraordinarily rapid changes. A massive Wan Chai freighter is gliding around the headland that falls down from Mount Davis and the *Ever Useful*, part of the Evergreen Line, is steaming into view. There is constant motion on this waterway.

From the steep hillside above rise several slender apartment towers, the pale blue and white buildings of St. Clare's Girls School, and a cantilevered house inspired by the spare lines of the Bauhaus, replete with tall rectangles of glass and steel. Cut into the side of the mountain both above and below Victoria Road is the Pok Fu Lam Cemetery, with its "Home for Coffins." As with the sports fields, there is here, too, a convergence of histories, of religions, of architectural styles. The dead, too, have their sense of taste, even if *de gustibus est non disputandem*. Each to her own in matters of taste, but Kant is not content with this formulation, all too facilely rendered in our age of self-infatuation and a laziness of thought. A *laissez-faire*, in the negative sense. Kant thinks the "subjective universal," bringing together two concepts that, for the most part, do not seem to fit together at all and therefore each negates the other. If an experience is subjective it is not universal, we tend to think, and if it is universal it is not subjective. Except in those mysterious matters of what Kant will call "reflective judgment" and of a hunger for the beautiful (which, for him as for Plato, though in a different manner, is irrevocably connected to the good).

All is water and all is wind. Arrangements are important. *Feng shui.* Thales is not stupid. He understands, like Kant although in a very different manner, that thinking and elemental materiality belong together and are always inseparable. Philosophy is just this curiosity, this sustained response to the scrawl of relationality. It is a wild perplexity that poses itself as a series of questions that must be elaborated upon. How is world gathered and dispersed? What does it consist of? What is time? What is space? How does language create meaning? How does one thing cause another or become another? What is the "I"? How do good and evil operate and is there a "beyond" of the two? What is number? How are points distributed? How does a curve operate? What is an impersonal transcendental field?

Thales, like us, knows the world to be a differentiating whole and to conjoin materiality, thinking, living, and dying. The legend has it that, staring at the stars in the night sky and not watching where he was going, he tumbled into a deep well. Sky and earth; light and darkness. We all too often try to be certain about where we are going, step by step, but we are always distracted, looking elsewhere. A beautiful young woman laughed at him as he followed the arc of wonder and fell into the depths. I am not sure what the tone of that laughter was, though that would determine what sort of person she was and how, later, the two became friends.

Philosophy, with its tremendous powers of fascination and focus, becomes absent-minded about what is right in front of it. Philosophy carries with it its own blindspots which it then projects out on the world. But this is only part of the story and there will also be the movement of natural philosophy into the mathematics and specializations of the natural sciences, and, later, a resuscitation of attention to the apparently simple objects of everyday life that will come once again under the scrutiny of the curious eye of philosophy.

The sun is higher in the sky and the temperature is rising. A flock of birds—their wings barred with white—rises, wheels over the ocean, and returns to settle in a tree near the pool. The world is motion. The heat and humidity are stunning. The young children in pink and purple bathing suits, already begoggled, are learning to kick, hold their breath underwater, awkwardly (like the young amphibians they are) to splash from three feet out back to the edge of the pool. Their parents sit in the concrete bleachers looking on, slightly proud and slightly anxious. The children are learning through pragmatic actions like kicking, breathing, and screaming to be in the world, an aptitude required of us all for as long as we live. The world demands learned action and unconsidered responses to new situations, a practice of movement that entails ignorance, fear, excitement, friction, bruises, wounds, dying, and exhilaration.

Thales and Kant are both interested in the great philosophical question of *form*. How do individuated things emerge, become articulated, and pass away? Pools, goggles, umbrellas, kickboards, ships, mountains, the sea, the birds, the children, the sky? And, beneath or between such differences, what, if anything, abides? What connects the whole of space across time and time across space? How does the hyphen operate in the dynamism of the one-many-many-one?

Thales cannot explain how water changes forms and yet remains the same—he cannot yet invoke the chemical bonds of H_2O—but he thinks analogically from how he observes water performing to how he understands the world to be performing. The world is water. (And this "is" is itself magnificent.) Thales thinks analogically, with everything resembling everything else at some level of its activity. How do we draw out connections? What is conjoining? Philosophy is *ana-logos*, not just the *logos* as syllogistic logic or the logical arguments of an already established rationality. It moves along the strange loops, the deadends and the unexpected vistas, of the *ana-*. Philosophy is *physis* sive *poēisis*.

Kant is sitting poolside, slightly stiff and quite uncomfortable in his summer Prussian suit. But he's taking it all in by this promontory that drops into the sea on the western edge of Hong Kong Island. The man doesn't miss much. Thales is laughing as the *Ever Divine* appears and sails past Aberdeen, Cyberport, and then around Green Island, heading for the inner harbor to unload its cargo from the far corners of a world without corners. The heat, the water, and the city bring with themselves the ghosts of philosophy.

§

The Main Building at the University of Hong Kong, built in 1911, is located in the mid-levels where Caine Road meets Bonham and houses the philosophy department. I sit in the bliss of the air-conditioned office, loving the polished wood, columns, tiled floors, and beautiful round fountain of the old building. My office, tucked behind the copying machine, boasts doors of frosted glass, fluorescent lights, bookshelves, a metal desk with an old phone, and the air-conditioner that hangs from the ceiling around an old large-bladed fan.

The "is" is magnificent. The "is" is always splitting itself, ambiguous and proliferating. The "is" is many. We do not know how the "is" moves back and forth between the "is" of identity and the "is" of metaphor (to put it poorly). "Kant writes in German" and "2+2 is 4" are examples of the first; "the iris is a galaxy of birds" an example of the second. Even the second seems to make a certain type of claim of identity, but it is something other than the A=A of the first. It may also be the case, however, that A=A is not as simple as it looks and that the concept of identity or equality always contains within itself radical otherness. Difference; multiplicity. The iris—and is that a flower or a part of the eye?—is not a galaxy, is it? And, yet, in the sentence, they are conjunct.

The subject is and is not the predicate. This is a logical contradiction for ever since Aristotle we have been assured that A=A and that A cannot be not-A. Truths, things, sentences, propositions, or judgments are either one thing or another. Themselves or not themselves. True or false. Ding, ding! Many philosophers sneer at logical contradictions as meaningless drivel and not worthy of the least consideration. Non-sense. Meaning, they contend, is always linked to the truth-statements of logically consistent forms. And the meaningless, or absurd, can and should be completely overcome, cast aside, and obliterated. It endangers the very project of certain forms of philosophy. As for myself, I continue to listen to the hordes of bees that have long been invis-

ibly humming along the boulevards of tomorrow and pay attention to the quotation marks of perhaps.

Kant is shivering a bit in the corner, sitting in a wicker chair, as
if he is suffering from a slight fever. He mouths a single phrase:
"The synthetic a priori." I had thought he might mention this. I
will return to this central enigma, but, for the moment, I want to
stay with the absolute enigma of the "is" for a while longer, at
least until the moment of my death. (Does Kant ever use the
word "death"?) There is, perhaps, nothing else to think about, or
with, than the "is" and its shadow-double, the is-not.

The "is" is a sea, calm and pellucid. The wind is a labyrinth full
of blood and bones, the stench of a bull's breath. It is an image of
joy amid the holly and ivy of the greensward. The "is"—and its
double-shadow—allows the doors of the world to swing wide at
each instant, opening to the bamboo scaffolding around the new
buildings, the cranes that line the port, the marinated jelly-fish at
Lin Leung Tea House at G/F 160-164 Wellington Street (reserva-
tions: 2544 4556), and the sound of minibuses, taxis, and double-
decker trams rumbling buzzing and rumbling down the street. (Is
this perception or imagination? What is the relationship? What
does each have to do with writing?)

The "is" is simple: an "i" and an "s." A short vowel followed by
a voiced "s": zzzz, as if it is sleeping, dreaming. A dreaming copu-
la: ist, est, etc. But to place the definite article "the" before the
"is" is to nominalize it, to reify it into a what. Such a move sets us
on a long peripatetic path of philosophy in which the "is" and the
"thing" become confused. This is, perhaps, the entire problem of
ontology, the logos of being, or, if we nominalize it, the being of
be-ness. The "-ing" is more appropriate, more appropriating.

Early in the evening, the Hong Kong Observatory—at 134A Nathan Road, the long street that heads from Victoria Harbor north, bisecting Kowloon—raised the Black Rain Warning #8, the signal that a typhoon is approaching from far out in the South China Sea. This one is named Koppu, but I have no idea how the naming system for storms works in this part of the world. Excited and a bit anxious, I piled my books and papers on my desk and hustled out of the office to catch the 10A minibus and head back to Tam Towers. The city, of course, had dealt with typhoons a thousand times. I haven't. The rain was just starting to splatter down when I reached the flat and the winds were barely puckish.

As the evening darkened into night, however, the winds picked up and struck like a fist as the rains slashed across the black heavens. I sat at the window and looked out over the balcony at the storm storming, at the "is-ing" of the storm. I fell asleep at last, but around 3am the storm woke me with a jolt. The trees thrashed wildly, twisted around the bent axis of their trunks. The wind whistled like a wild wounded bird and the rain charged fiercely against the windows. Out in the bay, the sea was a tumult and the ships lay anchored facing into the wind and the waves. By the new light of morning, the rains were still falling and the winds were still blowing hard, but the force of the storm has passed on by. At 10am, the Observatory warning was lowered to a mild #3.

Kant paced excitedly to and fro as the storm raged. This is something he recognized. We were never in any real danger in this tower of concrete, glass, and steel, but he knew from his secret night rambles in the Prussian countryside across the flat plains outside Königsberg—when the neighbors were all tucked in their beds—how powerful nature can be, how it can tear apart the human soul and wreck a human life to the point of its destruction. An absolute destructivity, mindless, lies at the calm and silent eye of the roar of the typhoon.

The old Chinaman of Königsberg loved the thunderstorms that rumbled across the night sky that exploded with lightning. After furtively peeking out to make sure no one was about—after all, he had a reputation to maintain and had to uphold the good name of thought—he would quietly step out of the back door of his house and wind through the alleys and side streets until he crossed the river over the ancient stone bridge. The sky and the fields opened up to the expansive spaciousness of his sensibility. He tried, but failed, to keep from running, his arms spread wide as the rain soaked him to the bone until his whole body shivered. He leaned his face toward the rain and laughed with utter abandon. The storms caused him to shout out his greetings to the wind and water (although he would, almost simultaneously blush at his own unconstrained exuberance).

As the storm abated and the clouds passed raggedly over the face of the moon, he would return the way he had come, quietly re-entering his home, from whence, come a decent hour of the morning when common sense would once again govern the faculties, he would step outside—his stockings having been adjusted with the small machine tucked into his pocket—and greet his neighbors with a small nod as he headed for the university. The earth smelled of the wet night. Always, he was thinking, but sometimes thinking is a form of shivering. Kant began to explore this experience that broke through all the boundaries and exceeded all the categories: the "sublime."

Kant opens the "Analytic of the Sublime" in *The Critique of Judgment* by noting that the "beautiful and the sublime are similar in some respects. We like both for their own sake, and both presuppose that we make a judgment of reflection rather than either a judgment of sense or a logically determinative one... (CJ 97). These judgments, quite strangely, are "*singular* ones that nonetheless proclaim themselves *universally* valid for all subjects, though what they lay claim to is merely the feeling of pleasure and not any cognition of the object" (CJ 98). The universality of feeling must, therefore, be different than the universality of cognition. We have an experience, whether of the beautiful or the sublime, and this experience is idiosyncratically our own. *I* am experiencing *this*. On the other hand, and simultaneously, this feeling is universal for all of us. *We* enjoy this; *this* is beautiful.

We like the wind coming down from the Dragon's Back and skittering through the streets of Tai Po; we enjoy the sun, the darkness scattered with stars. We find the neon signs blazing in the Mong Kok night pleasing in their form. All of us. We do not know more about the world of scientific truth when we walk down Wellington Street—I cannot communicate my experience in a formula, in a logical syllogism, or as a repeatable data set—but we are cast out into the seas of pleasure. *A singular universal.* There will, apparently, be a need, though, for a way to establish connectivity between my idiosyncratic experience and yours. How do we not only touch each other on the surface of things, so to speak, but actually share experiences of individualized pleasure? We are, as it were, alone together and together alone. What, then, is communing, communication?

Kant wrestles with this question like Jacob with the Angel. *Sinnesempfindung*: not just sensation, but the *sense of* sensation (CJ 157). A sensation or perception that involves a sense organ: smell, touch, taste, sound. Kant knows that it is not the case that everyone senses the way I do and vice versa. You smell a rose differently than I do and it is possible that someone has no sense of smell at all. And, I may love the scent of the rose and you might despise it. Perception is not universal. Kant then leaps to the "moral character," for which "liking is not a pleasure of enjoyment, but one that arises from our spontaneous activity and its conformity with the idea of our vocation. [This] requires concepts and is the exhibition of a law-governed, rather than a free, purposiveness....the only way it can be communicated universally is by means of reason, and, if the pleasure is to be of the same kind in everyone, it must be communicated through quite determinate practical concepts of reason" (CJ 158). Perception is passive and singular and the moral law is spontaneously active—it must be if freedom is to be put to work—and universal? At this point, the ideal of universal communication depends on it being a function of concepts, practical reason (since it has to do with the moral law and not speculative metaphysics or scientific cognition), and "bound" rather than "free" purposiveness.

And, yet, neither of these types of experiences—perception or cognizance of the moral law—is quite the same as the experience of the "sublime in nature" (CJ 158). Beauty has to do with "boundedness," the form of an object—*that* building, *that* flower, *that* book, *that* man, *that* woman—while the sublime can also be "found in a formless object, insofar as we present unboundedness, either as in the object or because the object prompts us to represent it, while yet we add to this unboundedness the thought of its totality" (CJ98). A typhoon is approaching Hong Kong. In the experience of the sublime, the experience of pleasure is always "indirect" and produced by the "momentary inhibition of the vital forces followed immediately by an outpouring of them."

The sublime contains in itself both the attractive and the repel-lent. Such experiences are "incommensurate" with our power of representation, and, as it were, violent to our imagination, and yet we judge it all the more sublime for that. There is something about us that loves being-wrecked, something that believes that only by being torn asunder can we ever accomplish the reconsti-tution of ourselves that is morally required.

§

Pacific Coffee Company. "Come on, baby, light my fire," croons the recorded ghost of Jim Morrison over the speaker system, ubiquitous these days, whether on an iPod, a smart phone, or, as it is now, emerging from the speakers carefully placed around the Pacific Coffee Company Café on Wellington Street above Manning Drugs (one of the two drug store chains in town, the other being Watson's). Music accompanies us everywhere, whether in public or in the privacy of earbuds playing a person-ally selected playlist set on shuffle. The sciences of recording change almost everything. The sound of the voice, once the do-main of the absolutely private and ephemeral, is now changed utterly. Not only is the voice now made public and lasting, avail-able at the click of a button, but digital recorders can now pick up sounds not accessible to the non-prostheticized human ear.

The technological, as usual, breaks the limits of the physio-logical. We are mutating. The past infuses the present, warping its *chrono-logos* and the gothically vaulted halls of the palace of memory. We are all haunted by voices of bodies long dead that circulate around the world and out into the near-space of satellite orbits. Our own voices, if there is an "own" anymore, join in the chorus of the cacaphony. Jim Morrison, buried and flower-bestrewn in Père Lachaise in Paris, continues on auto-pilot through the days and nights of Hong Kong. Come on, baby. Light my fire.

Kant is tapping his fingers at the adjacent table, humming something quite unintelligible under his breath with an absent-minded look on his face. Thought distances us from ourselves and our immediate environs—it is always a kind of dis-place-ment—apparently occurring in an elsewhere from the here and now, though there is nowhere else to go. (Perhaps, freedom, and therefore all of philosophy, depends on this elsewhereness, this non-congruence of the empirical with itself?) And, paradoxically, it also brings us closer to something that is more foundational—and all of these words are dangerous—than the self itself. (What generates the "I" of the "I think"?) We look into the middle distance, as we think, and see nothing except for that mysterious empty space that invites thought to think.

A scent arrives on the wind and we begin pattering around, sniffing like a wild animal on the hunt, following an elusive track without knowing what will appear in the brush or on the high dry steppes. It is erratic, peripatetic, this thinking: this attempt to think the thought, to think any object of thought. We do not know how thought puts itself into motion, how it begins or how, finally, it orients us toward its own tasks that always, out of difference, bring difference in its wake. There is a kind of in-drawing as we detach ourselves, in thought, from the things immediately in front of us: the table, the coffee cup, the spoon, the glass of water, the other café aficionados, the fire that the Doors keep lighting. Kant is lecturing, he is walking, he is sitting in the Duke's library, he is jostling along on the MTR toward Kowloon Tong, where he will meet with other philosophers who are on their way from Paris, New York, Berlin, and Beijing. He is focused, with a free-floating attention, on an inward object-in-motion. Like the rest of us, he writes to slow thought down to the speed of reflective perception. Otherwise, we are completely outpaced and left in thought's wake.

What image do we have of Kant? For more recent philosophers like Nietzsche who exist after the advent of photography, we have all those photographs of the eagle-crested pale green *Haus* in the Engadine, his voluminous moustache, his fat and ugly sister, the last apartment in Torino. Nietzsche comes to us along with the brood of his family, the pastors all dead, as a series of images on silver-gelatin, film, and now in high resolution pixels. Kant cannot come to us quite like that, since he was dead by the time Joseph Niépce invented a way to store light and shadow in the 1820s that he called *heliography* (another name for which is *metaphysics*). The first photograph is the "View from the Window at Le Gras," and windows, with all that they bring with them about perspective and transparency, cannot be separated from everyday life in the city with its arcades, its apartments, and its skyscrapers. We do, though, have drawings, paintings, engravings, and descriptions of Kant, who always appears to be a quite serious and sober man, peering deeply into the intricate workings of philosophy. Kant, unlike our contemporaries, never made it to YouTube and Facebook. He is, or would have been, grateful for that anonymity, for such self-exhibition would never pass the test of the moral maxims, much less the objectivity of the categorical imperative.

Nevertheless, Kant waits for us as we head along the path into what is called "the future," looking absent-mindedly back in our direction as we try, in vain, to keep up with the slow speed of his thought. Niépce, by the way, used lavender and bitumen—isn't that related to the bricks that were used to construct the famous tower on the Plain of Shinar?—in his process of sun-writing. These two apparently unrelated details can go a long way to unearthing the desire of philosophy in its idealist forms: to ascend toward the heavens of pure knowledge with the light of the sun as a guide. Philosophy as heliography. Kant is a bit more modest than this and keeps firmly in mind the distinction between the "transcendent" and the "transcendental," between dogmatic metaphysics and critical philosophy. Out beyond the borders of the map, there are dragons basking in the sun with their scales shimmering on rocky islands and then sliding into the water to dive out of sight into the trenches of the seafloor.

Kant arrives, thinks, walks, writes, attends dinner parties, and dies. More than most, he is able to keep the long train of his thought moving along the track of the rational, for the tracking of thought provides an essential dimension of the architectonic of reason. At the end of the line of logic is the *telos* of reason: the trustworthy knowledge of science (*contra* Hume and all those other nasty skeptical empiricists) and the autonomous free will of practical reason, which, indeed, is more fundamental than any speculative function of reason, since without freedom there can be no such thing as "knowledge." And, perhaps, there is another kind of *telos* at work in history and art.

As Kant argues, "morality first discloses to us the concept of freedom, so that it is *practical reason* which first poses to speculative reason, with this concept, the most insoluble problem so as to put it in the greatest perplexity..." (CPrR 163). The understanding of nature, i.e. science, can always work on the assumptions of causality and the precise accuracy of determinate judgments, but it can never, so to speak, step back from itself and determine its own essence. It cannot measure the freedom which grants the foundation for knowledge. At that point, reflectivity and a different kind of knowledge—we might as well call it philosophy—comes into play and this, too, could not occur without freedom working its work. One of Kant's definitions of freedom is the "form of an intellectual causality" (CPrR 199), but the causality of the will and of the natural world of appearances are absolutely differentiated from one another. Another definition of freedom is "absolute spontaneity" (CPrR 219), since everything in the sensible world is interlinked as an effect of another cause (and is therefore bound, unfree).

Thought, when it is thinking, disturbs nothing and disturbs everything. It is profoundly quiet, folded silently into itself. It is as if we are asleep in the silent and motionless landscape of a great-hearted night. The moon and stars are quiet; the forest looms out of the blackness around us. Perhaps there is the sound of a creek flowing in the distance or the quiet hoot of a hidden owl. This is the thought of the earth and the sky; it is essential and we cannot do without it. At the moment, this thought is in great peril, and if it comes to an end, so, too, will human life on the planet. And for us, the thought of the earth and the sky is also the thought of the city, for "nature"—with which Kant is so deeply fascinated—is not a dichotomous other of "culture." Each is always folded into the other.

The thought of the city swarms with people moving like a river, like a glacier, like a cloud along the sidewalks, streets, up and down the escalators, and along the pedestrian passageways both above and below the ground. The city is an immense excavation of the earth, a having-been-moved of the earth, a displacement that has uprooted the contours of the land with its hosts of other populations. The city is a slow, steady explosion that creates a furrowed wound in the earth in order to establish its own apparent order. This is the finite order of human habitation, especially in the age of dynamite, bulldozers, and planning algorithms. It blasts out the side of a mountain and fills in Victoria Harbor; it creates an artificial island for the construction of Chek Lap Kok, Hong Kong's airport; it paves and wires the earth for the construction of a platform for digital and genomic mutation, with the hope of immortality humming like white noise in the background.

The Temple of Tin Hau, the Goddess of Fishermen and of Sailors, is now an MTR station stranded on a street far from the shoreline on the border between land and sea to protect the men who risk the water. The city moves the goddess away from her rightful domain and she must now learn to be also the Protectoress of Pedestrians and Elevator Riders. The thought of the city—which is inseparable from philosophy and its *agora*, its public spaces of articulation, persuasion, politics, and *eros*—is also, like the thought of the earth, essential, even if it is newer, more fragmented, and faster than the pace of the thought of the tree, the bud, the turtle, the paramecium. Both forms of thought, however, disrupt the illusion of the orderly movement of the architecture of logic, which itself must be undergirded with something other than itself, a something that Kant can only call the *a priori* or the supersensible *Ding an sich*, the thing-in-itself, but whose cognitive content must ineluctably remain absolutely empty since it is the unknowable that serves to found the knowable.

This enigmatic interface is Kant's portal, on the one hand, between the sensible world of appearances and the supersensible world of the thing-in-itself; and, this portal is also an interweaving between the two domains. "For, it is our reason itself which by means of the supreme and unconditional practical law cognizes itself and the being that is conscious of this law (our own person) as belonging to the pure world of understanding and even determines the way in which, as such, it can be active. In this way it can be understood why in the entire faculty of reason *only the practical* can provide us with the means for going beyond the sensible world and provide cognitions of a supersensible order and connection, which, however, just because of this can be extended only so far as it is directly necessary for pure practical purposes" (CPrR224). Tin Hau, for Kant, cannot open up to the divine since she is only in the empirical world of religious enthusiasm, temples, incense, and fishermen. Only the form of freedom can be the rational opening to both knowledge of the world and assurance of the moral world beyond sensibility that never comes into visibility as such. But this is a bit too much for me on a hot afternoon. I need an iced coffee.

Pacific Coffee is unthinkable without both the thought of nature and the thought of the city, which are folded together in the medium-roasted Arabica beans whose brewed form I am now enjoying. Along with all the commodities for sale here—the sandwiches and muffins, the mass-produced quiche lorraines, waters and juices, bags of coffee and shiny coffeemakers—there are, as always, photographs gracing the walls: two large black-and-white prints of two pairs of very elderly European men and women who are standing in front of some Cathedral or another. France, I imagine. The English on holiday during the heyday of Empire. Perhaps it was, at one time, a single photograph that has since been cropped in two. Both men and women wear hats, one of the men carries an umbrella, or a cane, despite the sunniness of the day. The dry leaves of a parched tree appear along the upper edge of both photos of the quartet that is long ago dead, buried and decomposed: but here they are, again, tutelary spirits that preside over all of us as we drink coffee and eat cake on Wellington Street. Silently and without seeing, though appearing to see, they greet us and take us west toward Europe and back into the vanished past whose tremor is still sensible.

I greet them as well, from an unbridgeable distance, and salute who they were when they inhabited space and time. I am as fleeting as they were and I, too, will soon be gone, greeting others via my image but unable to communicate in-the-present. I, too, will become image, memory, then nothing. Someone else will occupy this corner table and write other thoughts, of other thinkers. S/he, too, will look ahead and behind, try to look around the corners. Thought will continue on its meandering paths, heart-broken as always, but always learning again to give itself in the double affirmation of a "yes-yes," to tap at the table absentmindedly and follow what has been set in motion, to see what surprises us as it appears. Someone else will listen to Jim Morrison and the jack-hammers outside; someone else will sip the coffee; someone else will feel, beneath the stones of the street, the MTR tunnels, the sewers and the water pipes, the excavated earth, and, deeper down, the swaying of the sea. Kant, though, has not budged. His eyes are half-closed and his quill hangs loosely in his hand. A slight smile plays around his mouth. He is here and gone, absent and present.

§

The Kadoori Institute, a lovely retreat center in the steep hill country of the New Territories, is used for ecological research and for group gatherings. The pillars at the entrance and the square at the end of the hall frame the trees, the mountains, and the sky. Not as a whole—the sensible can never give us that—but as this particular scene, this particular portion of the world in motion. Outside the window at this particular moment—as if there were such a thing—the slow flutter of the leaves (I wish I knew the names of flora and fauna, but they never stick for long) against the deep green ruggedness of the mountain. Most people never think of this territory as part of Hong Kong, but here we are.

In fact, "Hong Kong" is something of a floating signifier, sometimes naming the island, sometime the city as a whole—including Kowloon—and sometimes the whole of the territories that, over the years, were stitched together in negotiations between the Chinese and the British. The opium wars, an expression of pure greed, shape the way we use language today. My friends and I spent the day, having been picked up by a big bus outside the Peninsula Hotel, getting oriented to each other, to the tasks ahead of us for the year, and to the context of Hong Kong higher education.

At night, the air is thick with humidity and the cooking fires are crackling away as, sweating like delighted pigs, we begin to learn our way around a new cuisine, all sorts of meats and fish. It is like an adult summer camp in the smoke and heat of fire and the thick scents of food on the grill. Walking back to our sleeping quarters, the lights in the valley below stutter in the distance and the black heft of mountains rises from the north. For the first time, as the half moon rose into the hazy sky, I feel the immensity of China looming behind me over the dark ridge.

When we all take the bus back into the city—refreshed by knowledge of all the universities and by our emerging friendships—we head over to Manning House, Queen's Road Central. A lavish Chinese banquet is being hosted by Po Chung, the visionary and funder, in partnership with the public universities, of the Fulbright Program in General Education in Hong Kong. After an extraordinary banquet at which the food just keeps on coming, he talks about a "design for life" and mentions Robert Pirsig's *Zen and the Art of Motorcycle Maintenance*. In particular, he focuses on Pirsig's distinction between the Classical and the Romantic as ways of understanding and living in the world. The Romantic, to grossly oversimplify, sees the surfaces of the world and the sheen of its beauty. The classicist, on the other hand, sees structure and function, the underlying architecture of the world.

The motorcycle is, of course, both, but most of us can fundamentally relate only to one aspect of the machine: the smooth paint and the polished chrome or the design of the engine. Everything in the world is like this: something with an underlying form that appears to us, offers itself to our perception. The lovely black pen with which I write, for example, is manufactured by the Mitsubishi Pencil Company (PIN 02-200 BLACK; Bar Code #49 02778 91526; MADE IN JAPAN) and contains the great mysteries of manufacture, distribution, functionality, and the ways in which nature shows itself mediated as a "pen." Modernity, for its part, numbers each item it mass produces.

At this level, the technologist—the contemporary form of the classicist—has a great advantage over the romantic, for not only can she enjoy the smooth flow of the ink onto paper, but she can also understand the way everyday objects arrive and operate. There is, however, a small difficulty built into this scenario, for the one who knows how the pen operates may not know how the air conditioner or mobile phone works. The one who knows hydroelectric power is unlikely to know the genetic sequence of the lemur. And neither, of course, knows Kant. (Why should philosophy matter?) The world has become specialized, technocratized.

We must, Po Chung insists, create pathways of thoughtful practice that travel sinuously between the classical and romantic world. This is just what Pirsig and his protagonist, Phaedrus, do, and it is even what Kant, especially in the third critique, lays the groundwork for. It is no accident that the generation of the Jena Romantics emerges in response to Kant. Kant was gifted with one of the most powerful classicist-analytic minds the world has ever known, always making extremely subtle distinctions and driving toward a structural architectonic of experience. The boisterous crowd from Jena—Novalis, Fichte, Schelling, the Schlegel brothers—worried that once Kant had severed the faculties of knowledge, morality, and aesthetics that they would never be rejoined. Kant knocks Humpty Dumpty off his wall. Took a great fall. All the king's horses and all the king's men wouldn't be able to put it him back together again.

In general, they were right (so far), since for all of us now the technoscientific, always aligned with capital, has become the dominant social force in the world and has laid claim to be the sole domain of truth. If this is left in place, without contestation or development, the earth will experience the utmost disaster, not simply the end of philosophy, but the end of thought. Everything will simply take its place as part of the preset program, the grand set-up. We must preserve room for thought, an infinite and patient spaciousness that works, in writing and the other forms of representation, to learn to attend to what is at hand and to what is around the corner of the next street.

Kant divided the mind into "faculties"—understanding, imagination, sensibility, and thinking—and argued for a noumenal world of the unknowable but thinkable in its empty but necessary formality. He longed to understand the fundamental architecture of the world and the mind—the two are inseparable—but discovered that this very longing for understanding brought with it its own discontents, its own limits, its own amphibologies and antinomies. Reason, pushing and twisting reason, turns itself against itself. Thought flexes backwards. This is philosophy: self-reflection as self-othering and self-othering as thought. Kant struggles to establish the legitimate limits of thought, but these limits are always being eroded by constant wavework. The island is always changing shape and respect for philosophy requires that we ceaselessly exceed philosophy's self-established limits.

For Kant, the mind and the "external" world of nature remain a unity in each instant of experience and a unity as an image of a totality as an unattainable ideal. Both the freedom of practical reason of ethics—treating each person with absolute dignity, as an end in and unto herself—and the mysteries of "reflective judgment" of the aesthetic, which returns us to art, science, and nature through the "as-if" of the productive imagination, are absolutely essential to the odd twist of nature called the "human."

§

Wan Chai. I am learning what all city dwellers learn quickly: life occurs both as a nomadic swarm on the streets and in the hidden but accessible floors above street level. This latter is a different perspective for me, acclimated as I am to living close to the ground. The dirt and gravel road through the cedars, spruce, and fir back home on Whidbey Island has only a distant relation to these streets of Central, Western, Sheung Wan, Kennedy Town, Tsim Tsa Tsui, and Kowloon. A street is not a road; roads are not streets. Elevators are needed to get to the restaurants and banquet rooms, to offices and reflexology suites, to lingerie stores and hair salons, to millions of peoples' homes. As I have slowly begun to learn more about Hong Kong family life, another factor that determines the need for both outdoor and indoor living space is the average size of the flats. Three or more generations can live together, some sleeping on the couch with the TV always on. I wonder how much of one's philosophy depends simply on how much space on has in one's personal life as a child and as an adult? What were Kant's writing hours and habits? Where was his desk, his bed? How did he cope with his multiple failures to land a professorship? What were his tastes in food, women, men? How curious we are about those who write books and about the books themselves. What is a writer? What does it mean to "be written"? What is writing?

Kant is sitting across the street at a café, a Campari umbrella protecting his table from the sun. He doesn't do well in this subtropical heat and is utterly indifferent to any of our interests in his "personal" life. It's all there in the books that he struggled so mightily to write. He'll be catching the #28 minibus to Admiralty, then a quick MTR shot to Wan Chai, where there is an international meeting of arts and antiquities dealers at the Hong Kong Exposition and Exhibition Center, a lovely turtle-backed building that juts out into the harbor on reclaimed land.

Writing has recently appeared twice on the Hong Kong TV. First, there was a marvelous little documentary on NOW TV about the palm leaf texts that are used as a writing surface in a particular region in China. The villagers boil the leaf, pound it, dry it, then write on the surface and join the leaves together with a string to form a book. These are very ancient records of when the Indians first made the journey to China, bringing with them the first Buddhist texts. The other mention came in a remark about a Pakistani poet, who, when he came to this point of death—and death is always a sharpened point—cast his poems into a lake. Words upon the water. A disciple of the poet, however, had memorized the poems, so they were reinscribed upon a more stable sheet of memory. Calligraphy, surface, memory, meaning, and a trajectory of writing of philosophy and poetry that casts itself toward the future. There is nothing, certainly not philosophy, without writing.

I'll follow Kant to Wan Chai to take in the exhibit at the Cultural Center, then catch the Star Ferry across to Tsim Sha Tsui, have a drink in Harbor Place, and then hop on another ferry back to Central. I'll see if I see any incense floating on the fragrant harbor or any letters forming themselves in the intercalations of the incessant harbor chop. Kant, like most philosophers, doesn't speak much about writing. Why would he? Writing is, almost always, that which is taken for granted by philosophy and which is almost always assumed to provide a stable surface aligned perfectly with frictionless movement of the hand and fingers that offers thought a dynamically transparent site for the meanings of its own self-revelations. What was the paper made of in Königsberg? Certainly not palm leaves or strips of bamboo. How was the ink made into which the sharpened point of the quill was dipped time and again, undoubtedly leaving drips and blots throughout the manuscript as it scratched its way into the body of the paper?

The hand moves across the surface of the waters and philosophy appears magically on the page. It is a labor of love, a labor of suffering and exhilaration that oscillates in a wave form of varying velocities and force. It is always the tenacity of hard work, persistence, and blind faith in the effort. Philosophy has never appeared without stone and chisel, papyrus and stylus, paper and quill, palm leaf and brush, or keyboard and screen. This raises a host of difficult questions. In the section on the "Schematism of the Pure Concepts of Understanding," Kant is articulating the relationships between the schemata, the concept, and the image with the general question of "How, then, is the *subsumption* of intuitions under pure concepts, the *application* of category to appearances, possible?" (CPR 180). Such a strange question is only necessary for philosophy, since all the other sciences simply assume it to be the case and get about their work of knowing the empirical world.

The "third thing," which Kant calls the "transcendental schema," must somehow have a connecting link with both the concept and the empirical experience for there to be "application." The concept of circle must be connected to the plate on our table; the concept of triangle must be connected to the diagrams and plans of the architect or engineer. While, of course, the image is available to us in the empirical world, the schemata is possible only in thought. If Kant cannot keep these two soldered together, he will regress into either Platonism or Humean skepticism, that Scylla and Charybdis between which he is incessantly navigating. This connectivity is, for Kant and for the rest of us, a great mystery:

This schematism of our understanding, in its application to appearances and their mere form, is an art concealed in the depths of the human soul, whose real modes of activity nature is hardly likely ever to allow us to discover and to have open to our gaze. This much only we can assert: the *image* is a product of the empirical faculty of reproductive imagination; the *schema* of sensible concepts, such as of figures in space, is a product, and, as it were, a *monogram* of pure a priori imagination, through which, and in accordance with which, images themselves first become possible. (CPR183)

The a priori imagination is "simply the unity of all the manifold of intuition in inner sense, and so indirectly the unity of apperception..." (CPR 186). It gives our empirical experience "significance"; it orders the world into a meaningful whole. To say that there is no philosophy without writing is simply to repeat Kant's claim that there is no thought, for human beings, without a connected sensible experience and we are all written on water.

Kant returns to this image-idea of the monogram when he is contrasting the "ideals of reason" with the "products of the imagination." No one, he repeats, "can explain or give an intelligible concept of them; each is a kind of *monogram*, a mere set of particular qualities, determined by no assignable rule, and forming rather a blurred sketch drawn from diverse experiences than a determinate image—a representation such as painters and physiognomists profess to carry in their heads, and which they treat as an incommunicable shadowy image of their creations or even of their critical judgments" (CPR 487). This is where the *Critique of Pure Reason*, with its hope for legitimating knowledge and the possibility of science, opens up to the *Critique of Judgment* with its strange universality that is based neither on rules nor on knowledge, and which is concerned with art, the beautiful, the sublime, and with the question of teleology in the natural world.

There is, apparently, experience without a rule to govern the experience. There is a *Schattenbild*, a shadow-image, instead of the heliographic light of pure reason that presumably shines neutrally on all things. There is a monogram—a squiggle, a doodle—that is intimately aligned with a personal style and with the very possibility of perception and cognition. Our initials are mysteriously in-scripted on experience in general. Freedom wraps itself in the folds of mechanism and the law is set free for justice, form opens toward beauty. We sign ourselves.

How do we read the monogram; how do we read philosophy or travel writing; how do we read Kant? In most instances, there is an unspoken assumption that an incrementally progressive reading, a reading undertaken by a single individual with the utmost assiduity or by a series of experts across hundreds of years, will some glorious day be finished as it completes the task by finally getting it right. The reading will completely absorb, and thereby obliterate, the writing. We will *understand*. The text, once its resources are absolutely exhausted, will be transformed into the clarity of understanding. The hunt will be done, at last, and the skinned hide of the writing can be nailed triumphantly over the crackling fireplace of philosophy. Given enough time, and the continuation of reading—which is in no way guaranteed— then one of us, at last, will have mastered at least one piece of writing: perhaps a critique, perhaps a paragraph, perhaps a sentence? Certainly never a word, as if a word could stand on its own. Writing-reading-thinking is infinite. It is infinite because it is finite; it is finite because each reader is time-bound, and therefore bound to and for death, and because of all the historical contingencies that bear upon the act of reading, say the A and B versions of the *Critique of Pure Reason*. I have limited capacity for knowing the history of the book's production and reception; for producing a new writing that serves as a form of response for a thorough reading; limited language abilities in both German or English, and, quite simply, limited intelligence. I am not as smart as Kant, so cannot read the texts from the same spot from and in which they were written. But even Kant couldn't understand his own *Critique,* since the reading Kant and the writing Kant are different Kants appearing at different moments in the weathered constellation of history punctuated by that great, and therefore multiply fissured, thinker we call "Kant." Reading is always self-dividing and this is an interpretive chasm that cannot ever be overcome. Kant, like every writer, is multiplicity. My own reading will one day stop breathing, but others will have taken up the endless task with a sharp intake of excitement and a patient determination that keeps returning to the pages of Kant in winter and summer, whether in Hong Kong or in Seattle, whether in a coffee shop or in a red bus hurtling through the streets of the city.

Even if once again reading retreats into monasteries, now with access to data banks and e-books, it will continue. Why? Because reading is the approach our own lives take toward that of an other and of the other toward our own modest space of living. This is the *sine qua non*, the necessary requirement, for us to understand the movement of our own lives as interlaced with the lives of others. To carry the lives we have been given, and life is always given, means to be carried toward the other by the othering within. Reading and writing, which produce philosophy, is the practice of this di- and nocturnal current of exchange.

§

Mt. Davis. The sun is rising above the shoulder of the small mountain enfolded in the city and above the offices, apartments, and schools set into the hillside. The hostel is newly renovated and ready to welcome travelers from all over the world. Yesterday, I travelled out to the Chinese University of Hong Kong, taking the 10B minibus down to Central to catch the red MTR Tsuen Wan line, picking up the green Tiu Keung Lung at Mong Kok, then switching to the rail line at Kowloon Tong toward Lo Wu, which sits on this side of Shenzhen, on the border with the mainland. The transportation in the region is extraordinary, though the need to get off the major transportation grid is growing and I may need to walk on a sandy beach soon. I've also been a bit more anxious riding the minibuses later at night, when the drivers are exhausted, exacerbated, or both. The driving patterns mirror, almost, the pattern of walkers, as everyone follows the flow in and out, streaming along to fill all open spaces.

There is a clear protocol on the roads: the big double-decker city buses have right-of-way with the minibuses trawling along behind them. There is very little room for error, but there is also a clear sense of order. When the roads are open, the minibuses speed around the curves carved into the mountainsides past the huge cemetery built along Victoria Road—and stretching up to Pok Fu Lam—with row after row of grave markers covering a great bowl scooped out by nature and by great earth-digging cranes. From the road, whether driving or walking, I can make out the black-and-white photographs attached to the gravestones peering out at me from an instant of their lives now long ago vanished, looking at me from the place of death with a calm and dignified gaze.

When they were alive, they were looking into the camera as if toward the face of death and now that gaze is reversed, looking, as it were, backwards. They are looking from their past into my future at the moment of the present. As if from a sheer blank wall and an absolute unknowability. Pure reason fails at this limit; there is no knowledge, whether through science or intellectual intuition, of death. There is, however, an *encounter*. Death, like and unlike the noumenon, is an x alongside all human represent-ability, a nothing that exerts causality on the close side of phe-nomenality where we stand in the hot sun and speak with one another. Time passes: all appearances pass away, but the form of time remains and other appearances appear.

Freedom offers itself once again in the midst of law and phi-losophy pushes beyond experience toward the highest pinnacles of thought. For Kant, *holiness* is the complete unity of the self with the moral law, which is the *highest* pinnacle of being, but this is impossible for each and every creature at each and every moment of our limited lives. We cannot know the whole and we cannot be the whole (since Kant rejects all types of absorptive mysticism). We have the idea of holiness, but nonetheless are also aware that we could only become holy only if we were to be granted endless progress toward this goal. "This endless prog-ress is, however, possible only on the presupposition of the *exis-tence* and personality of the same rational being continuing *end-lessly* (which is called the immortality of the soul)...a *postulate* of pure practical reason (by which I understand a theoretical propo-sition, though one not demonstrable as such, insofar as it is at-tached inseparably to an a priori unconditionally valid practical law)" (CPrR 238). There is a "postulate" of immortality, but it can-not be "demonstrated." We want to live forever, under certain conditions, but this is something we can only hope for (or learn to dissipate such a hope).

The photographs on the gravestones beckon to us, call upon us to think. Death, the non-depictability of the absolute non-object, is nonetheless indicated by these photographs on the inscribed markers on Pok Fu Lam that I cannot read. A legible illegibility, much like the neon signs in the midst of the city. A face of a person I will never have known reaches out toward me in a silent and shuttered greeting. We do not speak each other's language and we do not share the same history, but, nonetheless, we nod toward each other as we pass. We both know the form of the transcendental aesthetic of space and time. We both know how to use the "I." We are ineluctably drawn toward death but without being able to say anything about the "what" of death. It is nothing. It orients us, terrifies us, drives us to get things done while there is still afternoon light falling on the rounded shoulders of Mt. Davis.

§

The Travelator is a quarter mile long escalator, the longest in the world, that runs from the lower levels of Central up along Shelly Street to the Mid-Levels, passing through the bar and restaurant district of SoHo as it goes. (The name "SoHo" itself travels smoothly between New York, London, and Hong Kong, bringing with it the aura of the bohemian and urban chic.) Travelling down during the morning commute and back up after 10 am, the travelator comes in extraordinarily handy in the subtropical humidity that blankets these hills of concrete. It opens up a whole set of commercial possibilities for those who otherwise wouldn't bother with, or couldn't physically handle, the vertical angles. It must have been a massive engineering feat, one that accompanies the MTR lines blasted from underground, the tunnels from one side of the island to the other, from the Hong Kong to the Kowloon side of the harbor, and the foundations for the soaring skyscrapers and new piers reclaimed from the harbor. Hong Kong is a built environment par excellence.

A moving sidewalk is an oxymoron. Stand still and move along: the acting out of a paradox. This isn't Zeno's paradox, however, for one easily reaches the top of the escalator and the O Café without any intellectual gymnastics or knowledge of the limits in calculus. Zeno, of course, never had any trouble arriving at the market in Elea or at Parmenides's house. One foot in front of the other, or, simply stand still and let the travelator whisk one up the hill. Zeno just thought it all; thought it odd that objects, like an arrow, can move through ever smaller units of space that can always be divided and sub-divided, infinitely. How does movement occur if, as it obviously is, such is the case? The ordinary world is not as it appears. The simplest "fact"—we can get from a to b—is infinitely complex. Might not the thought-world and sense-world be at odds?

Philosophers and their friends also know that one can step off the escalator at Lyndhurst Terrace or Hollywood Road without any problem at all. The Peak Bar or Cicada—with their luscious steak mint dish—is easy to reach for a drink or dinner. Buying a pork bun at the 7/11 or a ordering a falafel to go are not challenging undertakings that take much thought. Refuting Zeno is not necessary for the daily round to work and pragmatism tops idealism every time we start longing for a hot, fresh bun.

The ordinary is the ordinary. It is stiflingly hot outside. The ocean looks like it is moving in many directions at once as the

Hapag-Lloyd ship churns out past Lamma Island and disappears. Each day, and usually very much in passing, a host of swarming thoughts and sensations cross our minded bodies. I worry about small pains and wish I didn't have to die. I already miss the world that will be when I'm gone (though that raises difficult questions as well about world-constitution and the individual ego, passive and active syntheses). What are my unborn children like? Who might I have been other than who I am?

There are small yellow and red blooms in the trees; the red taxis stream up and down Sha Wan Drive; the railing on the stairs up to the street feels warm to the touch. Ordinary day, ordinary events. There is nothing behind the scene and the curtains will never be magically lifted to reveal the real world behind the apparent world or to show us the secret that governs all comings-and-goings. The play of the world shimmers across all the folding surfaces of the scene. The silhouette of the mountains—and silhouettes fascinate me—is etched across the edge of the sky and merges into the hazy blue of the sea.

The shimmer, as it incessantly flutters, produces the possibility of meaning, of identities, of continuities, of history and futurity, of desire and fear, and of the many ways in which language works to touch the shimmering. Kant, who in general would like to slow and finally affix the shimmering into moments of a shared objectivity, speaks of the conditions necessary for the possibility of knowledge, of the freedom of practical reason upon which the possibility of ethics and, indeed, of speculative philosophy depends, and of the odd aesthetic universalism of reflective judgments. He speaks of the regulative ideas of God, the Self, and Immortality, all of which are necessary for thought but can never, under any circumstances, become objects of knowledge. As he will never tire of saying, "all thought must, directly or indirectly, by way of certain characters, relate ultimately to intuitions, and therefore, with us, to sensibility, because in no other way can an object be given to us" (CPR 65). Only that appearance that is related to sensibility can become an object of knowledge and all immediate experiences of true intuition are sensible, not intellectual. There is no direct vision of the real, for human intelligence is always "discursive," bound to the unfolding sequential form of time. One step after another.

There is, for Kant, no intellectual intuition of the Idea(s). Without our sense organs and the body as body, there would be no such thing, for human beings, as knowledge. But the body is accompanied—and the choice of the word that will occupy this place in the sentence is always inadequate—by the understanding of the mind. The case of the matter always concerns itself as sense-understanding, body-mind, in which the hyphen is always an active, and unknowable, mediation of what Kant at some points calls the synthetic work of the productive imagination. While there certainly are Ideas in the Kantian sense, they are always the work of reason and not sensible understanding, and, as such, set limits and are themselves the limits of thought.

The ordinary is the ordinary. The ordinary is not-ordinary. The not-ordinary is not-ordinary. The not-ordinary is ordinary. First there is a mountain; then there is no mountain; then there is a mountain. Philosophy requires the bustle of Hollywood Road, the stunning heat, the movement up and down past SoHo of the travelator. But the travelator also requires philosophy for the rocky ride of understanding to occur. At mid-day, the heat is shimmering off the boiling pavement.

§

Hong Kong Island is divided into three regions: the watery domain of the harbor with its churning waves, its pollution and waste; the posh Mid-Levels and the constant push of traffic picking its way along Bonham, Caine, or Robinson Roads; and, at the top overlooking the rush of misery and happiness in the lowlands, life on the Peak, the country of the taipans and the walk along the Dragon's Back. Hordes of tourists take the funicular from the Garden Road station, across from the US Consulate, up to the Peak's observation station with its shops and restaurants, but few make it to the Peak to live their daily lives, for it is the home of serious Hong Kong money and historical connections. *Guanxi.*

The ancients divided the world into the Underworld, Middle-Earth where all of our mortal lives transpire, and the realm of the gods in the sky above. Zeus: Sky-Dweller (and he is a late-comer). Kant's philosophico-geography is different since by the Enlightenment, Isaac Newton—and not Homer, Sophocles, Plato, or Augustine—is the presiding figure. Kant divides up the world of the faculties of the mind into the senses, understanding, reason, and that strange capacity called the imagination. Nature is the totality open to the sensible intuitions of the understanding, while reason always wants to push beyond the appearances of nature to the whole, a move that, though inevitable and necessary, can yield neither knowledge nor mystical illumination. It is the world of pure thought that produces its own limits, the antinomies of reason in which contradictory positions on the fundamental questions of cosmology run aground.

As the mind listens to "the voice of reason within itself, which demands totality for all given magnitudes...if the human mind is to be able even to think the given infinite without contradiction, it must have within itself a power that is supersensible, whose idea of a noumenon cannot be intuited but can yet be regarded as the substrate underlying what is mere appearance, namely, our intuition of the world" (CJ 111). Reason, on its own, has a voice. The inner voice of the human is a voice of reason. (Can the voice of reason only intone and proclaim, or might it *sing*? If so, what are its beats and rhythms, its tenors and timbres? Its snap and swing?) The supersensible, which cannot be known but enables all of the conditioned world to be known, brings along with it an image, as it were, of the totality of the world as world.

Always so vigilant against the mystical enthusiasts, Kant diligently labors to keep nature and the supersensible distinctive from one another, reminding us that "the idea of absolute totality concerns only the exposition of *appearances* and does not refer to the pure concept, such as the understanding may form, of a totality of *things in general*. Appearances are here regarded as given; what reason demands is the absolute completeness of the conditions of their possibility...What reason prescribes is therefore an absolutely complete synthesis, whereby the appearance may be exhibited in accordance with the laws of understanding" (CPR 390). Understanding, which is what the empirical knowledge of the sciences rests upon, must be complemented by the ideas of reason for there to be an "accordance" of mind and object.

Kant, as always, works very hard *both* to articulate the trustworthy operations of the understanding *and* to delimit the power of pure reason as it attempts to come to grips with "the absolute totality in the synthesis of appearances" or the "world-whole" (CPR 385). In this he is, simultaneously, extremely ambitious and extremely modest in his aims. He wants to recognize "transcen-

48

dental illusions" while not falling into skepticism or despair, to situate thinking in its proper realm between Plato and Hume. Such vigilance, Kant asserts, certainly

> guards reason from the slumber of *fictitious* conviction such as is generated by a purely one-sided illusion, but at the same time subjects it to the temptation either of abandoning itself to a skeptical despair or of assuming an obstinate attitude, dogmatically committing itself to certain assertions and refusing to grant a fair hearing to the arguments for the counter-position. Either attitude is the death of sound philosophy, although the former might perhaps be entitled the *euthanasia* of pure reason. (CPR 385)

Reason can be euthanized, but critical awareness keeps us from claiming too much for its powers, to act as if we were gods, and it also keeps us from falling into the position of complete despair over the fact that not only do we not know anything with finality, but, because of the lack of linkage between the mind and nature, we cannot ever know anything with finality.

Kant defends the "sound philosophy" that walks the middle-way between the extremes of dogmatism and despair. This is, for him, philosophical health, while the two extremes lead only to the pathologies of thought that are, finally, based on a lack of understanding of the nature of the "I" and the objective conditions of the mind and its knowledge. There is no world without mind; no mind without world. Skepticism and dogmatism misunderstand this relationship. These "antinomies of reason," the places at which reason inevitably becomes snarled with itself and oversteps its bounds, occur only in the realm of what Kant calls the transcendental ideas or cosmological concepts, not in everyday life, ordinary logic, or in the discoveries of the physical sciences.

"The antinomy which discloses itself in the application of laws is for our limited wisdom the best criterion of the legislation that has given rise to them. Reason, which does not in abstract speculation easily become aware of its errors, is hereby awakened to consciousness of the factors that have be to be reckoned with in the determination of its principles" (CPR 395). Critical vigilance awakens reason to consciousness of itself and its capacities as well as its limitations. Reason can, however, act without awareness of its own principles. Usually, in fact, it does just this.

A sound and healthy philosophy is aligned with a "law for our limited wisdom" and a "criterion of legislation." Kant, as always, is writing within the discursive field of the judge, the law, rules, and legislation: the world is *governed by just law*. But if the understanding that governs the knowledge of appearances and of reason becomes wrecked on the attempt to establish its own grounds apart from experience, *what guarantees the validity of the vigilance for the law of limits that Kant invokes?*

The traditional cosmography of the ancient world was tripartite: the world of the dead, the world of the living, and the world of the gods, who do not "live" as mortals live since it is our mortality that makes us so keen to live-on as best we can. In Hong Kong, these three domains still exist, but now they are side by side along the streets with the joss sticks offered to the gods and to our loved ones who have preceded us into death. Philosophy, as it orients itself, draws a line through a series of points and, in versions like Kant's, those points become an arrow that points toward the Peak. Plato, and others, have thought the Peak accessible. Kant, on the other hand, bows to necessity and the limits of human rationality and argues that the Peak—as the source of being that we can trace back to through a series of causes or as the thing-in-itself—is out of reach, forever withholding itself. It is pure withholding, pure reserve, pure outside. How does the resplendence of the world shine? What is this highest good that Kant names the holy?

Logic is a paring knife that separates the wheat—the nutritious kernel of truth—from the chaff, the detritus of error, illusion, and untruth. Philosophy cannot exist without logic in both its formal and informal sense, but logic has, in the late 19th and throughout the 20th century, made a valiant effort to leave philosophy as metaphysics behind, or, more often, to claim the entirety of the name of "philosophy" for itself. Logic is the travelator, carving its way up and down the hillsides; it is the system of the MTR and tunnels burrowing under the earth and water. Through making correct distinctions, cuts in being, and through the correct application of rules, we are enabled to travel toward the Peak, accumulating shiny nuggets of truth to hold in our palms as we go. The ridge becomes steeper, sharper, in the bright sunstruck day. One step at a time, but everything is linked and the timed steps are set into motion together. The logician, of course, cannot just enjoy the ride to the top of SoHo and get off for a cup of coffee at Café O. He must know how the travelator works—that will be called "technology"—and toward what it runs, as its end. This will be called "teleology" and that will have metaphysical implications, regardless of what the logician thinks about metaphysics or the technologist thinks about means and ends.

How does the rational abstraction of logic configure with the so-called "data" from the empirical world of the senses? What makes all these cuts? The west has given up on *feng shui*, wind and water, though it is still actively practiced around Hong Kong, where one must insure that the residence or business or grave has its back toward a mountain and looks out toward peaceful water. That will guarantee prosperity, for "water" sounds like "wealth." There are rumors that the angles of the Bank of China, I.M. Pei's magnificent building, were designed to cut into the power base of Norman Foster's HSBC Headquarters Building, which it faces, as well as the Legco, the legislative center inherited from the colonialist Brits. Others complained about Pei's angles and all the "X" shapes involved in its design. *Feng Shui* and the modern sciences of architecture. Computer Aided Design and Business Information Modeling: the digital platforms which create the physical presences of the skyline. How do the two co-exist in the same space in Hong Kong, where money and people flow like a turbulent wind driving hard across the harbor? No wonder the body of the earth is slashed and burned. How might we create the city as a form of well-being?

§

The Chung Yeung Festival, also called the Double Ninth, is one of the ritual days when Hong Kongers visit the graves of their ancestors, wiping the dust and grime of the year off the engraved stones that mark the place of the dust of the remains of those whom we have loved. This is the site of mourning, perhaps the accompaniment to each and every one of our memories, since memory always carries with the lingering effects, as affect and image, of the "it was." Experience is cracked along an infinite number of fault-lines, which allows the swirl of renewal to occur incessantly.

It is fitting—and what a word this is—that Chung Yeung occurs in the fall when even here in the subtropics the weather breaks. It is a bit cooler now, and, thanks be unto Tin Hau, the humidity has fallen off a bit. The winds, too, are shifting from arriving in the city from the South China Sea and are beginning to be primarily from the northern mass of the mainland. This will bring hazy clouds of particulates and pollution—Hong Kong's pollution problem is becoming more and more severe—but, for now, the birds are chirping and tiny red blossoms are appearing. This feels like a kind of new life, this autumnal pulsing of time, but it is related, as usual, to a passing away as well. Whidbey Island, our home on the North American side of the Pacific Rim, is wet, cold, and cloudy by this time of year, but in both places, separated by so many differences, there are yellowed leaves curled on the ground.

The men, women, and children arrive in busses, mini-busses, and taxis, coming from the island, Kowloon, the New Territories, and beyond to stand at gravesites on Pok Fu Lam, wipe the dirt away with clean water and enact the ceremonious rituals that honor the ones who have passed but are nonetheless present for the visitors. As I walk from Sha Wan along Victoria Road as the cemetery spreads out on the steep hillsides on both sides of the road. The mountain rises to the right; the Lamma Channel and the outlying islands spread out to the left. Each gravesite marks a hole in the world that will never be filled, but each gap also evokes memories not only of each individual and all that we'll never know of their lives, but also of ancient China, Egypt, the Neolithic, and the earliest funerary rituals of Cro-Magnon and our lost cousins, the Neanderthals. This hole in existence marks the presence of the human.

A butterfly, blue along the wing-edges, shimmers in the dap-pled sun as it flits among the greenery and then flutteringly soars up among the buildings in what must be a strange combination of disorientation and ecstasy. With an exquisite elegance it floats along the micro-currents of air in its hidden vortices, arabesques, and velvet pockets.

Everyone buys bouquets of flowers splashed with whites, reds, and yellows and carries them gently to the plinths of the graves. Flowers: the perennial symbol of new life, of the blos-soming of life alongside and out of death. Roses, narcissi, white lilies, chrysanthemums, red poppies, and asphodels sacred to the goddess of the underworld. Architecturally, the grave is reminis-cent of a house or a temple which holds the spirit of the ances-tors, loved and feared, served and supplicated.

One middle-aged man bows to the black-and-white photo-graph of his mother. For a long while he stands, in his simple black trousers and creased white shirt, in a firm but relaxed pos-ture, looking intently at the image of his mother's face. Perhaps all the questions of philosophy are gathering in this moment? He does not look away, nor does she. Then he bows, slowly and with decorum. Three times. I, in turn, bow toward him, slightly and inconspicuously, and continue my walk along Victoria Road, past the shirtless flower dealer and past the Home for Coffins, toward Sandy Bay, where I will loop down toward the sea.

Halloween in Hong Kong doesn't seem unusual at all, since we've been visiting Tin Hau Temples with all the masks of the goddesses, gods, and dragons at the doorways, gracing the rooflines, and inside the altars. Dragons are everywhere and the hike along the ridge that bisects the island is called the "Dragon's Back." Kowloon comes from *kau lung*, nine dragons. The Hungry

Ghost Festival occurs in August, at which money, food, and other offerings are made to the restless dead to keep them in their place. Eat! Eat! And, on my way back on the ferry from a reception on the aircraft carrier USS George Washington, a major business figure in Hong Kong educated me about some of the basic principles of *feng shui*. Make sure, he suggested, that your house always looks out on calm, and not rough, waters, backed of course by the strength of the mountain. Halloween seems a natural for Hong Kong.

None of this reads as the tired old concept of post-Enlightenment "superstition," which is inevitably set against monotheistic-scientific rational norms of truth. (What is really superstitious for us is the irrational belief in the rational–choice model of the market.) *Feng shui*, ghosts, the goddesses who protect the land or the sea are all examples of the basic rituals of human life, different ways of establishing relationships with the elemental powers of the earth, the sea, the dead, justice, and living in right balance.

Halloween: masks, costumes, candy. The ghouls roam the earth. The sweets are tricks or treats, gifts to the costumed ghosts, the children practicing being others, knowing already that they are always others. The pre-formed plastic faces of superheroes, monsters, pirates, vampires: the whole fabulous and fabled panoply of the underworld come to the surface, wandering Lan Kwai Fong and Pok Fu Lam, wandering Nathan Street and the New Territories. The thin elastic band with the straight metal clips on each end that, stretching around the back of the head, holds the mask in place. One use and it's done: trash. Who wants to be the same character two years in a row?

Soon enough the social norms will bear down very hard to rigidify the personality and its roles; the "persona," from the Greek for "theater mask," will harden into a "character" and into "sincerity," "authenticity." The children will forget, for the most part, how to play, how to change costumes. Art will recede to be replaced by calculation. Kant has a problem. On one hand, there is the absolute freedom of the will, the will to will of the will. On the other, one must will that which is universal—the categorical imperative—and that is a limit on the will. Make-up provides another type of mask in the world that is entirely make-believe, founded on faith in theater. Cosmetics open a cosmos that is full of glamour. Now there is no gap, not even the gap of the mask, between face and otherness. The face is the other becoming-other. Look at yourself in the mirror: what do you see? The only universal is universal strangeness. My face is bloodied, scarred, streaked, smiling a Cycladic smile, painted with a clown's black tears and an ecstatic joy.

Does the costume support the face or the face the costume? They match, of course; there is a certain fit between face and clothes, the clothes of the trickster. Night begins to fall and the goblins begin to scamper up and down the flats seeking offerings from open doorways. Then the older children and the teen-agers, a bit self-conscious but secretly delighted to be out, emerge. Parents, a bit anxious but wildly in love with their costumed scamps, stand in the background, guarding the herd of spirits and heroes. Kant has his own theory of disguise, illusion, and dissimulation, but within the world of knowledge it is based on a theory of similitude of mind/world and of phenomenal/noumenal, while in the world of pure reason it becomes the ineluctable transcendental illusions generated by the necessities of reason itself. Reason creates its own swarms of spirits and Kant will consistently strug-gle with whether the world is "as-such" or "as-if." I prefer the lat-ter, which gives rise to the former. But I might be wrong.

The phenomenal world is the world of appearances, which are all of the possible objects available to all possible human beings (or other rational beings from distant galaxies). There can be a "world" only for consciousness, for consciousness has reflexivity as one of its essential characteristics. Without consciousness, without rational beings, the world vanishes. What, then, are these so-called "objects"? The football, cricket, rugby, and tennis going on at the Stanley Ho sports center. The yellow and orange jerseys of the opposing teams and the low hum of the vending machines. The stain on the concrete floor and the chattering of the birds invisible in the nearby trees. The minibuses chugging by and the slash of a brownish green that is the sea. The weather in Seattle or on the planets circling Arcturus; the histories of the coffee cup and the Book; my sorrow that accompanies loss or my anticipation of new discoveries; Proust's description of Balbec and all the swarm of ghouls, goblins, ghosts, and ancestors that are focused around Chung Yeung or All Souls. And if, one day, we are to meet our cousins among the stars, there must be a similar-ity of a cognitive-communicative structure. We must share the same mind, the rational order of the world. I have high hopes for that meeting.

All possible experiences under all possible conditions of space and time. All that the senses can perceive, the mind think, re-member, hope for, fear, regret, repeat, imagine. All of this is available for the empirical experience of consciousness, but, for Kant, this is insufficient. All of this, even though it's an infinity, is not enough. There can, for Kant, be no empirical experience at all

without a transcendental field of the a priori conditions of experience: the transcendental aesthetic, a transcendental logic, and
the categories and schema that, as it were, provide a mediation
between the transcendental forms of thought and the empirical
contents of experience. Kant distinguished general logic from
transcendental logic:

> General logic, as we have shown, abstracts from all content of
> knowledge, that is, from all relation of knowledge to the object,
> and considers only the logical form in relation of any knowledge
> to other knowledge; that is, it treats of the form of thought in
> general. But since, as the Transcendental Aesthetic has shown,
> there are pure as well as empirical intuitions, a distinction might
> likewise be drawn between pure and empirical thought of ob-
> jects. In that case we should have a logic in which we do not ab-
> stract from the entire content of knowledge. This other logic,
> which should contain solely the rules of the pure thought of an
> object, would exclude only those modes of knowledge which
> have empirical content. It would also treat of the origin of the
> modes in which we know objects, in so far as that origin can be
> attributed to the objects. (CPR 96)

Reading Kant is difficult. A little bit here, a little bit there. The
hope is that there will be a painfully slow accumulation of understanding while, at the same time, recognizing his inconsistencies
and the final impossibility of a "correct" reading. Though there
are a multitude of partial and incorrect readings, there can never
be, finally, a correct reading. It is possible, in other words, to say
"that is *not* true"—if a judgment does not accord with general
logic that we are familiar with—but not quite possible to say,
with an absolute certainty, that "that is true."

Transcendental logic is the "other logic." It is, as it were, the logic of logic (and here comes the Third Man careening into view). Thought is always already divided into the two logics, the one "pure" and the other "empirical." The former, transcendental logic, "contains solely the rules of the pure thought of an object" and "treats of the origin of the modes" of knowledge. Rules and Origins: this is transcendental logic. It is the logic of Reason that oversees the logic of the Understanding. For Kant, it acts something like a linchpin, a joint, a little spiked button that holds two pieces of cloth together.

Why does Kant need this overseer of the understanding? Because experience, all experience, is constantly in *flux*. If flux is the final word, there cannot be, finally, any predictability, causality, teleology, or, actually, any *knowledge* at all. Hume, Kant's *bête noire*, is the one who teaches him the most. The black beast of skepticism is always lurking close by to any idealist form of philosophy, ready to spring. It has very sharp claws. But, as we also know, the beast is always accompanied by beauty, though that beauty may long remain hidden. Kant will, of course, speak quite openly, if not always clearly, about beauty as it draws him on, like reason and freedom, beyond the bounds of knowledge.

Knowledge requires regularity and regularity implies predictability. The world is such that rationality can identify and make use of the "laws of nature." Cause creates an effect. Sunrises keep occurring, day after day. The oak tree never produces the unicorn. Rain falls down, not up. One, two, three, four: death is knocking at our door. Nobody comes back. Every action produces a reaction. All of this seems to work pretty well. We get medicines that work consistently; the Mars Rover lands on Mars and not on Jupiter; when I decide I need a coffee at Pacific Place, I expect the café to be there when I arrive (and, so far, I haven't been disappointed, though capitalism will certainly continue in its "creatively destructive ways and the café might one day not be there").

Rational ordering works as planned; it programs its results that depend on a program having been set up prior to the results being produced. This is a discourse on method. Science tends not to worry about itself, but philosophy, like an anxious parent, always worries about science and its costumes. Hume is the hobgoblin on Kant's shoulder, always whispering into his inner ear: "Just because it's happened this way before, doesn't mean it will happen this way again." The empirical world, on its own, gives no guarantee of the reliability of knowledge. General logic, on its own, can give no final guarantee either, since it is emptied of all content but cannot justify itself within its own domain. (Gödel walks through Königsberg and Hong Kong.)

It is November, winter back in Seattle, and Hong Kong is still baking beneath the sun. Down Sandy Bay Road there is what they call a "village." It's a small ramshackle ensemble of lean-tos, metal roofed shacks, laundry lines, and potted red flowers that are worlds away from the shiny wealth of Central or Admiralty. These are lives I will never know, lives for which it would be worth learning Cantonese to understand. The traffic moves slowly along the road, back and forth; the waves saunter into the shore as the sun sinks slowly down toward the mountains of the western horizon. Everything is in flux; the world is motion. Illegible legibility.

§

Hollywood Road in mid-morning, while waiting for my fitting appointment with Ranooni Bespoke Tailor. This time of day is gorgeous, soft with sunlight and full of both restfulness and pos-sibility. The day is here, and good, and the day is yet to come. Other parts of the city are already in full swing as I took the mini-bus down past Dragon Faith Realty and Joy Ocean Massage. Wind and Water. The Dragon. Here on Hollywood, though, we're still at that quiet moment before the shop doors clatter up to re-veal the storefront windows and keys turn in the locks as propri-etors step inside to rearrange the desk, to straighten out exhibits before the wandering shoppers begin to arrive.

This moment of an unfolding, like a fan, of the instant that becomes the fullness of the day, is exhilarating, but calmly so. The moment of being-poised-for when each word of that phrase is pregnant with what might come. The buildings visible from the street are lit by the slanted sun but are also still emerging from the long shadows. There are dilapidated housing units with grime covered radiators, long strips of peeling gray paint, rusted air conditioners, and drying laundry. The tiny balconies, balconies in name only, are reflected by the shining new office buildings and condominiums of steel and glass.

There are many moments in Hong Kong when one sees reflec-tions on every side, as reflections reflect reflections. (The taxi stand on Peddar Street is a particularly illuminating spot for these reflections.) It's a delightful, slightly frightening, and extremely provocative moment for thought. The simulacra producing other simulacra as I look on and become enfolded in the reflections. (Kant, of course, has a way out of this infinite reflectivity of rep-resentations.) The crumbling living quarters and the new offices bespeak different histories, economies, politics, and architectur-al dreams. Function and form; form and function.

The streets are becoming slowly busier, but not much, not yet. All of these people in Central, myself included, have been preceded and will be succeeded by a host of strangers. Hong Kong is an image of both the frenetic speed of capitalism and the haecceity of every human life. Everything comes and goes; everything leaves within itself a space of replace-ability. This is what facilitates the dynamism of the world, the very possibility of motion, and maintains the essence of the human as the site of the trans- and the meta-.

Once one reaches a certain age, one no longer sees a stable person in front of us, a friend or a stranger, a stranger who is a friend. Instead, we see the sequentiality of each person, and each object, that is projected backward to birth and forward to death. And, in some traditions, even "birth" and "death" are simply part of a larger series of karmic multiplication. We see the girl in the woman; the wizened and stooped figure of the old man that grows out of the boy; the corpse in repose, waiting to be deposited in the rows of crypts being prepared for them in the cemetery. The *Augenblick* radiates in all directions. The instant of space is shimmeringly resonant.

Walking down Hollywood Road toward the Man Mo Temple and then back toward Ranooni Tailors, I stop for a moment and sit on a metal mesh bench next to the travelator, wanting to write in the same manner that a painter goes to his sketchbook. Any place, finally, will do, since any place at all participates in its own quiddity that guarantees its own othering. We host, and are hosted by, an infinite host of parasites. The painter must take note of the world in its inimitable immediacy, its smooth roughness. The eye of the hand and hand of the eye trace the contours in which we are in the midst of. The peeling paint, the café, the door, the sunlight striking the windows and the walls. Art is the attention to the world as it traces us tracing it. Not reproducing, not mimicking. Reflection, perhaps, but only in a certain sense. It is time for my suit to get fitted.

The "fit" of things is a riddle. The jointures of the differentiated articulations of the world. For philosophy, perhaps, it is the only riddle and Kant spent his entire thinking life thinking about this. How is it that the world, with its infinite multiplicity—though a multiplicity that cannot be experienced by any single rational agent—acts as one? How is it that the world makes sense, is in many ways a knowable entity? How is it that language fits to the world? God? Evolutionary adaptation? Chance? *The sea is a wrinkled quilt of blue. Two men in yellow jerseys walk across the football pitch. The Ferrari eases its way past the cardboard hauler next to Happy Valley.* Riddle after riddle. Consciousness and the world. Ideas, knowledge, judgments, words, affect. The intelligible and the sensible; the scientific, the moral, the beautiful.

But, as we all know, the world is not a smooth machine that purrs along without a glitch. It is always in need of work, of renovation. We have to keep our tools handy and our hands trained. The glitch, with its friction and its snags, is essential, for it is yet another name for the basis of freedom and for the capacity for displacement that insures the changes rung by time. Just as we think the fittingness of all things, we also must think the un-fit, the dis-coherence of all things. Sin, suffering, sorrow, and death. Nonsense, the absurd. The bloody eye sockets of the face that waited on the side of the road, from before the opening page, for Madame Bovary as she drove the horses hard in her fancy equipage.

Kant is famous for drawing the distinction between "analytic" and "synthetic" propositions. The first are of the sort in which all the information we need is contained in the subject of the sentence and so does not really extend our knowledge of the empirical world (though they do raise a host of other questions). If we are going to learn more about the world, however—if we are going to do science that tells us accurately about the cosmos—we need *synthetic a priori* propositions. Philosophers, with all their nibbling and quibbling, are quite hilarious.

In a passage omitted from the B version of the first critique—and how fascinating it would be to write books composed only from the passages that Kant or Kafka deleted from their "final" versions—Kant notes that "A certain mystery lies here concealed; and only upon its solution can the advance into the limitless field of the knowledge yielded by pure understanding be made sure and trustworthy" (CPR 51). A certain mystery, indeed: the mystery that evokes thought as well as the desire, and the foiling of that desire, for the "sure and trustworthy." A step forward. This is Kant's version of the ancient philosophical dream of certain knowledge that can replace certain mystery. But since the field of knowledge, as he says, is limitless, the certain can never be synonymous with the exhaustive. The limitless breaks open every proposition about the determinate knowledge of the world and an equal sign will never be able to be placed between human knowledge and the possibilities of experience.

In analytic propositions, the subject A contains within itself the predicate B. (What, however, is the action of "containing"?) "All circles are round." The concept of circle contains within itself the concept of round. A=A. The negation of the statement will be false. "All circles are not round" and any additional predicates that do not belong to the a priori concept of circle will also be false: "All circles are periwinkle; all circles are fizzy." (This is the logic of poetry.) Synthetic a priori judgments, though, are different. B is not contained in A. A, as it were, opens up toward B without knowing what B will bring. There will be surprises. Analytic statements are ruled by the law of identity, while synthetic statements are ruled by the law of otherness, which is to say that they are ruled differently: unruled, disruled, misruled. There is, however, even in the analytic proposition, the need to "become conscious to myself of the manifold which I always think in the concept" (CPR 49). Even the analytic concepts which contain themselves within themselves are a complex field of consciousness, the multiplicity of the manifold, thinking, and the acts of relating all of these together. Perhaps they are not so simple after all.

In any case, Kant states clearly that "Judgments of experience, as such, are one and all synthetic" (CPR 49). The two types of judgment, then, are also aligned with "experience" and "not-experience," or with what philosophy had learned to call the "a posteriori" and the "a priori." Experience always outstrips concepts, even though experience can never assure us that the a priori judgments are correct. Divisions and distinctions, in Kant, keep proliferating endlessly, although he will also, and quite directly, address the thought of the whole. Kant uses the sentence "All bodies have weight" to serve as an example of a synthetic proposition, arguing that to discover the weight of a body, we must muck around in the field of experience. (How would you determine how much you weigh? Can you just put your finger to your forehead and think about it? Why not?) "While one concept is not contained in the other," Kant explains, "they yet belong to one another, though only contingently, as parts of a whole, namely, of an experience which is itself a synthetic combination of intuitions" (50). Kant makes me laugh out loud.

We experience something: say the weight of this smooth dark rock taken from the beach at Shek O that I now hold in my hand. (Can you see it? Can you feel it?) This is a complicated experience of contingency; we don't know ahead of time how much it will weigh or what that will feel like in our hand, but by exploring in the field of experience, we can find out. Although the predicate is not *contained* in the concept, it nonetheless *belongs to* the concept.

This, then, is a synthetic judgment, a judgment from and about experience. But now things get tricky and Kant introduces a third category of propositions he calls the "synthetic a priori." These are just plain strange. It seems like the two parts of the term should not at all fit together. The synthetic belongs to experience—it just means to combine perceptions into a synthesis of differences—and the a priori, by definition, belongs outside the realm of experience. How, and why, could they possibly be connected? Nonetheless, Kant feels it necessary to give it a go. Buckle up.

The key to understanding these strange beasts is the "necessarily belonging to" that occurs in some judgments of experience. Kant's example for this is his analysis of "Each happening has its cause." He argues that "each happening" and "cause" are distinct from one another, and the latter is not *contained in* the former. Nonetheless, for each happening we can *always* find a cause that *necessarily belongs to* it. "What is here the unknown=X which gives support to the understanding when it believes that it can discover outside the concept A a predicate B foreign to this concept, which it yet at the same time considers to be connected to it?" (CPR 51). This is a movement of the secret that exhibits great beauty as one concept links up to the otherness of a foreign concept, thus becoming connected to one another in a necessary and universal way without ever being merely bundled together in the identity of a single concept. Multiplication and unification are always engaged in intercourse. The world is erotic.

"Each happening has a cause" is not an analytic proposition because we must go outside the container of the initial concept and it is not simply a synthetic proposition since if we turn to experience we will *never* find either a thing called "cause" or the self-support required for understanding. Neither is a possible object of experience, but each is required for thought. *What supports the understanding?* This is an extraordinary question: what props it all up? Is a prop a foundational structure or a theater prop pulled out from the darkened wings behind the curtain so that the show can go on? Or, to use a more dynamic metaphor, what makes the show run at all? We are on the edge of the noumenal and the numinous is flickering along the frames.

Such propositions exhibit universality and necessity, the criteria for the a priori, but they are synthetic in that they amplify and extend our understanding beyond the logical truths of the analytic. They are not, however, regular synthetic judgments, which are both contingent and open to empirical testing for verification. (How much do you weigh, today?) Kant's entire endeavor to provide a critique of understanding and reason rests on this explication, for as he says, "Upon such synthetic, that is, ampliative principles, all our a priori speculative knowledge must ultimately rest..." (CPR 51). Only such statements lead to genuinely new knowledge. If we think that such is possible, with an equal emphasis on the "new" and on "knowledge," then we will stand with Kant against a pure empiricism, which cannot escape skepticism, and against the speculative rationalists who think everything can be unfolded out of the Idea.

The day is beckoning and I have had enough, for the moment, of the synthetic a priori. I'm in the mood for a walk, for a new blue suit.

§

Hung Hom Train Station. As I prepare to depart for Guangzhou and then Macau, I'm waiting beneath Starbuck's, Maxim's Express, and McDonald's. Fast food, like music and movies, travels around the world with ease. On this level are Circle K, Seven Eleven, Baleno, and Kam Kau Jewelry. The station is a space of crossings, transitions, arrivals and departures. Hung Hom becoming globalized and the world becoming Hung Homized. The currents of globalization run deep and strong.

As the preeminent thinker of Enlightenment, Kant was deeply engaged with whether the history of humanity is a history of progress or simply an "idiotic course" (UH 12), whether humanity has a noble goal of freedom and self-awareness for itself or is simply a "contemptible plaything" (UH 13) of nature. Does nature have a *telos*, a goal for itself? How could we possibly know whether we're living out a coherent narrative or only stumbling blindly along toward the final dead-end of evolutionary options? Kant takes on these questions in "The Idea of Universal History from a Cosmopolitan Point of View," a short essay published in 1784 in the *Berlinische Monatsschrift*. When he looks out at the drama of the world, Kant sees that almost everything is constructed from "folly, childish vanity, even from childish malice and destructiveness" (UH 12). (Sounds familiar, doesn't it?) All of us are making history in a blind groping ahead for immediate satisfaction and there is no sign of a plan in this primal scene.

It is no accident that Kant uses the figure of the child to represent the unenlightened individual and the unenlightened species. He had argued a month before he published "Universal History," and in the same newspaper, that Enlightenment is:

> Man's release from his self-incurred tutelage. Tutelage is man's inability to make use of his understanding without direction from another. Self-incurred is this tutelage when its cause lies not in lack of reason, but in lack of resolution and courage to use it without direction from another. *Sapere aude!* 'Have courage to use your own reason!'—that is the motto of the Enlightenment. (WE 3)

When we become enlightened, we leave childish things behind for a more mature and visionary action in the world. As if the child could be ultimately dismissed. Since our "tutelage" is self-incurred—there is no external authority demanding that we desist from thinking—then it's possible to step into our own rational sphere and inhabit our own authority. Once we, as individuals and as species, reach an "age of reason," then we have the possibility, but not the necessity, of becoming rational beings. Rationality, in other words, depends not only its own capacity but also on the activation of our freedom through "resolution and courage."

As Kant never tires of reminding us, the practical reason of morality and freedom is more fundamental than scientific knowledge and logic. Why? Because otherwise human actions, like other natural occurrences, would simply be following the "aimless course of nature and blind chance takes the place of the guiding thread of reason" (UH 13). Without the self-reflectivity of freedom, knowledge would be simple instinct like that exhibited by the bees and the beavers. But the operational activation of this freedom for thought depends upon certain affects, certain passions of the soul. Courage is the one necessary thing to escape from self-bondage and become enlightened as one who employs her own reason.

Autonomy, even if it is always partial, is the possibility of a gift that brings with it responsibilities toward the open-ended ambiguity of our lives. How does my freedom interact with yours? What is the "our"? What is the "self" and what does it mean to "govern" or "legislate" this self? It is through our enduring practice of responding to such questions that we develop the very capacities of which Kant is speaking. Autonomy of thinking requires practice in thinking; thinking, in turn, creates autonomy when put into practice. Truth emerges through acting within constraints.

Hung Hom provokes thought with its trains headed into and out of Hong Kong, with its history of industrialization enwrapped in global commerce. This is the city in action, the city in fast-food motion. Grab and go. Eat and run. Everything is a distribution network; everything on the move. Guangzhou, the factory to the world, awaits just across a border that is not quite a border. One country: two systems. The train is here; it is time to go.

§

The Star Ferry Terminal and Wellington Street. There is nothing better than the sun on the water and the sun on one's face, sitting on a bench near the ferry terminal. The world is warm and glittering. We bask in deep contentment, our faces turned helio-tropically toward the sun with our eyes closed against the bright-ness, but still seeing the red of the inside of our eyelids. This is beauty; this is the history of western metaphysics. The plaza is beautifully designed with its tiles, flowers, and small trees. Invis-ible birds are keeping time with the light breeze from the harbor. IFC/2 is visible just to the right; the skyscrapers on the Hong Kong Island side are dark blocks against the glare of the sun.

Reflective surfaces arrive on the reflective surface of my mind. The plexiglass barrier protecting the stairs up to the Viewing Promenade; the upper deck windows on the *Celestial Star*. Now *there's* a name for a boat: to navigate by the stars of the celestial sphere and its magnanimous order. We can orient ourselves to the fixed stars while the planets, those erratic and elliptical wan-derers, keep moving against the dome of deep space. The stars stay put, stay calmly set in their pre-established places so far away, so high above. A perfectly stable backdrop for the change-lings of history. So distant, so close, so clear. It is not only death that equalizes each of us, but also the sun on our face in late De-cember with the harbor a silver sheen bordering on black.

A police launch slips by; a helicopter hovers overhead; a man in a pressed blue suit walks purposefully by with his mobile cocked to his ear while another, in an old beige pair of pants and a windbreaker, taps his foot as he sits on one of the mooring posts. Then they are both gone. Couples, singles, and gaggles of pre-teens stroll by. The shadows are, though just barely, begin-ning to lengthen. The skyline begins to darken as the sun de-scends over the island though that darkness will soon be coun-tered with neon that will flicker up and down the buildings. The buildings on that side are casting their reflections into the harbor's waters and the afternoon softens for all of us out on the promenade, wandering the streets of Kowloon or headed on the ferry back across the harbor to the Central Pier.

The afternoon draws all of us into a sun-drenched motley crew with the shadows coming on. I wish I could know each one of them, listening in to their dreams, their fears, their hopes, the desultory chitchat that goes on in their minds. I wish I could *be* each of them, as well as their ancestors and descendants, and to know them singularly and simultaneously in order to know every possible variation of the human experiment, the human song. This is the old wish to be God and we know that Kant disallows the possibility of intellectual intuitions, much less this wish for transcendent unity of the mystic.

Kant works assiduously to keep the wall between the experienceable world and its noumenal source in place, for if the wall falls down then the validity of any empirical-scientific knowledge cannot be justified. If it remains impermeable, then the empirical world becomes merely a stage for knowledge without meaning and the grounds for a complete nihilism are laid down, waiting for the appearance of the man with migraines who moves to the Engadine before heading back toward sea-level in Torino. How, then, should we live?

Back in Central after disembarking from the *Celestial Star*, I drop for the first time into Segafredo's, on Wellington Street. *Une caffé per amico!* It's already Christmas Eve and the time in Hong Kong is progressing, slipping away. I had hoped to run by ReCycle to pick up a few gifts, but after walking down Caine to Elgin, the shop turned out to be closed. I'm now giving both sides of Wellington equal attention, since I so often hang out at Pacific Coffee across the street. A lovely warm ham and cheese baguette with a latte in a smooth porcelain black cup accompanied by a biscuit. After my respite, I head down toward Sheung Wan, passing the ornate frieze of red, gold, and green set into the front of one of the buildings. It looks like a representation of the zodiac, but I'm not sure. The emerging into consciousness of the frieze, however, also suggests another phenomenon concerning my capacity to see, to observe, to take note of, and to understand.

It's as if we have an inherent limit to the amount of stimulus we can absorb and retain—and the neuroscientists could certainly tell us something about this—for we very often have the experience here in Hong Kong that something new, yet something we must have retinally seen many times, becomes part of our awareness. The physiological unconscious that must be constantly streaming along but only at times images itself as consciousness. I walk along "Wellington," this complex amalgamation of British, Chinese, European, and material histories, a constantly shifting phantasmagoria of perception. Some things come into view while others vanish out of sight. I continue, of course, to imagine them there after I have walked around the corner; I continue to imagine the other side of the street and my destination in Sheung Wan.

"Wellington," then, is neither a stabilized neutral place "in" which people and cabs and carts come and go nor is it a jumble of disconnected particles of stimuli. It is an inextricably connected play, a constant dance that exhibits both patterns, consistencies, names-and-images, as well as a capability for incessant change in which one moment bows graciously and gives way to the next.

Hung Hom leads to the Star Ferry leads to Wellington and they all twist back upon one another, the city a complex of names, feelings, pressure on the feet, clothes stores, restaurants, histories. The Christmas holidays have arrived and the family is visiting from San Francisco. The airlines, like the ships coming and going from the South China Sea, bind together the Pacific Rim.

§

Beijing, the Ming Tombs, and the Great Wall. The extended family has all flown up to Beijing to see what it's like. An early morning mixture of fog and smog—I wonder if the words rhyme in Chinese?—hovers over the cityscape of the Wangfujing District and our lovely hotel. Outside, winter is coming down hard, brutally cold with bitterly cold winds sweeping across the city. The Mongolian steppes seem right outside the hotel door and Genghis Khan has become the north wind. We wander about taking in all the exotic foods—scorpions and sheep penises stick in my mind—and the vendors trying to make a yuan. There is some sort of theater nearby, massive boulevards of shopping, the Forbidden City with its frozen white moat and seemingly endless chambers and plazas, and the flat white expanse of Tiananmen Square, the symbolic center of Chinese power. But across a little side street from the hotel is the most beautiful find of the day: a local restaurant with giant steaming hotpots of food. I want to put my hands into the boiling water to warm them up.

Bitterly cold or not, however, we are in Beijing and the day after we arrive we hop on a tour organized by the hotel and take a bus out to the Great Wall at Badaling and then on to the Ming Tombs at Ding Ling. At the Wall, we make our way up the mountain paths and the frozen stairs to the massive parapets and then, moving as fast as we can in the useless but lovely winter sun, we climb towards the highest tower, which indifferently waits for us in the hard turquoise distance. The winter landscape is stunning;

the existence of the wall itself is sublime. (How many lives and deaths did it take to erect this enormous protective line of defense?) The mountains extend forever, but soon I begin to dream of hot tea. Steaming tea, scalding the tongue, with a white jasmine flower unfolding miraculously in the clear glass pot. With frozen fingers and ears, we stiffly climb back down to the rickety bobsleds on tinny rails that run us down the hill back to the moneychangers in their layers of winter wraps. I pay for a trinket and get some poorly forged paper money as change, walk past the souvenir sellers, the foul bathrooms, and inside to—blessed be they!—the purveyors of hot tea. Life's greatest pleasures are the simplest of all.

After a short respite of warmth we reboard the bus, listen to our tour guide extol the belief in the infinite existence of Mao's mummified and mausoleumed body, and then drive into temple complex of the Ming Tombs at Ding Ling, the Tomb of Certainty. In the site is a Gate to Paradise that the Emperor used to pass through. When crossing the threshold of stone, raised just a bit off the ground, he would intone "I will be back" in order to insure his return from the other side of the gate. He needed to let the ghosts and demons know that he wasn't, at least not yet, on the side of death to stay. There is of course no difference between one side and other—it is a frigid winter day with fragile, gleaming trees and hardened earth on both sides of the gate—except for the minute, infinite difference that the threshold itself announces.

When returning from Paradise to the usual grind of governing an Empire, the Emperor needed to lightly leap back over the raised threshold to insure that the hungry ghosts—and when aren't ghosts hungry for life?—couldn't follow him from the other side into the human realm. Apparently, ghosts must stay very close to the ground when they travel. We, on the other hand, need to always dance with light feet. The Emperor, then, and then those of us who are mere pawns in the game of geo-politics, each recites "I will be back." However it is that we come and go, and through all the multiple threshold crossings that we make from the living to the dead and back again, there is always the recitation of a simple declarative sentence. Across a possible infinity of experience, which bridges both sides of Paradise, the "I" remains, as does the verb set in the future tense. In the future, I will return.

Kant speaks of "transcendental apperception...a pure original unchangeable consciousness" (CPR 136). This is an astounding sentence and seems to contradict all that he says elsewhere about understanding, sensibility, reason, knowledge, and the ideas. Since all we can be aware of as an object of experience falls under the a priori categories, and is within the forms of space and time, how could it be that we have any notion, much less experience, of "pure original unchangeable consciousness"? It seems that this would provide the necessary ground and guarantee for self-consciousness and identity, for knowledge as a congruence between consciousness and all possible objects, and for the unity of the possibility of any experience at all. This is the miracle of unfolding of perceptions, whether on this side or the other of the Gate of Paradise. It is the fold between the internal and the external, which are simply two modes of the same field of consciousness called transcendental apperception. (Hasn't Kant just become a Spinozist?) It's an infinite field of creases, planes, knots, and crisscrossings, an articulated expanse of worlding.

It is not that there is no obscurity in the world; there, of course, is. What shall I do? How shall I live as I die? Where will my next meal, paycheck, or love come from? What if it doesn't come? How can I withstand the bleak wind and lusterless sun of the winter? But every instant of our confusion, despair, joy, and not-knowing are moments of the transcendental apperception of consciousness, unchanging and original. I have no real idea about how to understand this. Appearance + consciousness = perception. That is Kant's usual formula. Perception is linked to rules represented by the categories—causality, predictability, measurability, and repeatability—and becomes knowledge.

That there *can be* perception, understanding, and reason is the miracle. Moment by moment, we each leap back and forth across the almost negligible threshold that is a gate and not a gate, that divides the living from the dead simply by its architectural announcement of itself. The ghosts cannot follow our dance, and, frustrated, they take their leave to leave us to our play. How transcendental apperception works I will, out of necessity, leave to the great mystics of all the traditions. In the meantime, the hotel with its gorgeous heaters awaits our return. I will go in search of more tea and then crawl under the covers to read.

§

Catchicat Street and Causeway Bay. Back in Hong Kong after the Beijing jaunt, this morning I hopped on the 56 bus outside the flat and rode down Victoria Road, overlooking the Channel to Kennedy Town for a quick haircut on Catchicat Street, where we also have our laundry done at Cooper's, get our keys cut, and eat at the Clay Oven, an Indian restaurant. For these services, I pop my head in the door and mimic snipping my hair as I put on a questioning expression. English and Cantonese don't help, but the body language in the right context does. The questions are known ahead of time and almost no meaning needs to be generated. Snip? Yes. Sit. Cut. Comb. Mirror. Money. The End. That's the narrative line, prescripted by social habit and the pragmatic ready-to-hand knowledge of how to get along in the world in which hair, customary fashion, scissors, money, and chair coalesce into "haircut." Intuitions are gathered into a concept and a synthesis of the manifold occurs.

Since philosophy is the art of understanding and therefore the art of interrupting the prescripted, of veering off unexpectedly into another direction, in the direction of the other, not much philosophy goes on here in an explicit manner. There is, of course, a lot of that chitchat, if one knows Cantonese, that is so essential to oil and polish the social body called Catchicat Street, Kennedy Town, Hong Kong, and it is always interesting to discover how people talk about the scale of place to which they feel most attached. Philosophy is also a tiny step to the side or to the back in order to reflect upon chitchat, so there is a bit of that.

More importantly, there is an aquarium in the window of the barbershop. The water is full of brilliantly colored red, blue, and golden fish with gossamer fins as light as summer sails that luff along in a breeze as they undulate, as if weightless. Strollers on the street gaze in at the fish with delight, not really paying attention to the function of the shop, while I sneak a peek when I can while being snipped by the barber, a middle aged man with gray streaks beginning to appear in his black hair. Gazing into the fish tank as if it's another world, a watery otherness, people on both sides catch their own reflections and the reflection, however vague, of whatever is behind them, as they watch the graceful underwater spectacle of the bright-scaled fish.

After the haircut, I take the tram from Kennedy Town to the Causeway Bay turnaround and begin walking back toward Central from there among the bustling local crowd, not a *gweilo* in sight. This is one of the delights of being in Hong Kong; I am often one of the few Caucasians around and I get to learn a bit more about being in a minority situation, although I just simply *like* being in the Cantonese crowd. I walk by street-markets with the stalls stuffed with fruits, nuts, spices, dried fish, clothes, toys, and food objects I have no way of identifying. What are these things *for*? How can the same object be entirely banal for some and entirely exotic for others? Making my way to Lockhart Road I wander by the saunas and all the bathroom fixtures and flooring stores one could ever dream of. In the Causeway Bay Typhoon Protection Basin, multimillion dollar yachts, sleek in silver and white, are moored next to ancient sampans with frayed tarps bleached by the sun and rain. Along their edges are old rubber tires to protect the gunwales and men in shorts, sweating, are moving about repairing odds and ends.

The sampans are water taxis as well as living quarters. Mobile homes. One chugs up to the base of the concrete stairs leading down into the water and a man in a business suit climbs up the stairs and is gone, the boat already reversing itself. I have no idea where they originate or what their destination is, but I suppose it could be anywhere for these sea-people who know the waters around Hong Kong like the backs of their hands. The sampans and the yachts perfectly mirror the social disparities visible everywhere in the city, where the wealthy bankers and stock brokers stroll alongside the junkmen hauling cardboard out of deluxe luxury-brand stores.

Keeping the water on my right, I discover Jardine's Gun, originally used to salute the comings and goings of the *taipan* of Jardine & Matheson. (The silly things we do to mark status.) Now it's fired at noon each day and people who contribute to a charity called "Mindset" are allowed to fire it. Strange exchange, it seems to me. We'll do anything to be close to social power, even if it's a relic of the power of the past (though the gleaming white Jardine building, replete with its porthole windows, is visible from here as well). Continuing my trek down the harbor promenade, I soon run into one of those impassable cul-de-sacs of bridges and multi-laned roads with the traffic zipping along. There is always a way across, but it usually requires backtracking to a spiral overpass. It's hot and exhausting, but it does remind me to slow down and take my time, since there is no other way but to trek along. I catch the MTR bound for Central at Wan Chai, the station for the Internal Tax Office and the Chinese Visa Office as well as the local Délifrance on Johnston Road where we eat breakfast whenever we have official business to attend to.

At the Wan Chai Immigration Tower, my wife and I, when we arrived in the city back in August, registered for the HK identity card required of all residents. A small biometric machine recorded our left and right thumbprints and then we went up to the 8th floor, since our appointment had already been booked on the net. Several floors below us, Filipino and Indonesian women hoping to be hired as domestic workers waited for their turn to see the officers of the state. They would love to live in the servants' quarters on Sha Wan Drive, or, at least, they would be willing. Their families back home are waiting for the transfers of cash, which from Hong Kong total in the billions of dollars.

What's better than a visa and a baguette? KFC and McDonald's are close by, as well as Pacific Coffee and Caffé Habitū, but we are creatures of habit, and, while in Wan Chai we prefer French fast food. (There are also good ones in Stanley, Sheung Wan, and Mong Kok). One of the ways that expats like us stabilize our experience is to go to familiar fast food joints and to make the unfamiliar ones familiar. Globalization: mass production that looks the same in Cleveland, Santiago, Melbourne, London, Shanghai, Munich, Seattle, or Hong Kong. The reproduction of the same that gives us the mimetic comfort of a home away from home. Home as the Golden Arches. "I know who I am, wherever I am, as long as there is a Délifrance nearby. *Une croque monsieur, s'il vous plâit.* Language, like décor and cuisine, can play a similar role. *Prêt a manger:* a British quick-food company that speaks French around the world.

Hong Kong is drifting toward Beijing and away from London, drawn by the forces of geography, tradition, language, money, and, most importantly, national politics. But this is not a simple unidirectional tug from the motherland, for there has been a great deal of history—of both colonialism and democracy—embedded into the habitus of the city. (In another era, it would be a city-state along the lines of Renaissance Venice or the Hamburg of the Hanseatic League.) Yesterday, there were protests outside the Legco against the proposed plan to build a high-speed rail between Hong Kong and Guangzhou that would uproot villages in the New Territories. There have been regular protests outside the Liaison Office of the Central People's Government in the Hong Kong Special Administrative Region and the Victoria Park vigil for the Tiananmen Square crackdown of June 4, 1989, reaches over 100,000 people per year.

With PLA troops garrisoned, usually invisibly, in town and with the Bank of China, Citigroup, and HSBC all huddled together as they battle each other for market share and *feng shui* blessings, the city sits on a series of immense fault-lines, on a tectonic plate that slides over legal, economic, political, and philosophical fissures that could crack apart without much provocation. The stress, after all, has been building for a long time. The U.S. Navy is allowed in the harbor, refused entry, then allowed back in. The South China Sea is becoming a much dicier playground for military exercises; the Japanese are starting to build more submarines to counter the growth of the Chinese Navy; land prices are the highest in the world; and there is a huge gap between the yachts and the sampans.

Hong Kong is wealthy, operates under the rule of law in the British tradition, and is an essential cog in the machinery of advanced finance capitalism, both in Asia and globally. But Hong Kong is *small*. Singapore and Shanghai are close by. I would love to be able to know the fate of the city in the next hundred years, but one thing is certain, it will not be a fate of solitude and being left to its own devices. I get out of the MTR at Central. Coach, the luxury goods store, is across one street, Louis Vuitton across another. What a place, what a compression of human desire. I'll head for MIX, across from the old Central Police Headquarters, and a last cappuccino. (By the time this book appears, MIX will undoubtedly have disappeared.)

§

Cooper's Laundry. Cooper's has a nice new green sign, trimmed with gold lettering. Today I walked down from the flat—it takes about an hour—along Victoria Road, the sea and sky a bright blue. Quite warm as well: a delightful winter's day. Good, as always, to be in Kennedy Town with its lack of pretension. Lunch was done, shopping for the most part finished, so the streets were relatively quiet as everyone went about their Sunday afternoon business. Walking around the block, I noticed all the hole-in-the-wall restaurants. Simple tables and chairs, few decorations, the menus only in Cantonese. They are all delicious, I'm sure, as this is where the locals eat, tumbling out of their tiny flats. There are plenty of western eateries here as well—the Zig-Zag Café, the Italian specialty shop, McDonald's—but most of KT is local business in both food and otherwise: the barber, the butcher, the fish market, the keymaker, the laundry: workaday lives.

I have no idea where the majority of KT's inhabitants work, whether they stay close to hand or head down to other sections of the city (although it does get very crowded on the buses during rush hour, so many are headed elsewhere on the island or over to Kowloon). The massive container ships are all plying the waterways: MOL, Maersk, Evergreen, China Lines. A steady stream of seaborne traffic. They are piled higher with containers than back in August, a good sign of increasing trade and perhaps a signal of better times to come. The MSC ship headed back out to sea from the harbor at the moment is filled to the brim from aft to stern with only the highest level of the bridge visible.

Hong Kong loves to speak of itself as a "World City"—and it certainly is—but all of these "worlds" that converge in Hong Kong are not congruent or symmetrical. They sidle up to each other, cast their eyes this way and that; touch each other in a back alley, a mall, or a massage shop; idly eye each other in the IFC elevators; or walk by each other indifferently as they jostle across

Queen's Way or Nathan Road. Goods of all sorts, some visible and some not, are streaming around within the city and then out across all sorts of boundaries. Hong Kong is a city of spectacle—the light-show at night that dances across the faces of the sky-scrapers is the best example—but the spectacle of shopping, ar-chitecture, and fashion as well. Men and women show themselves in an enormous and sinuous promenade that winds through the intricate network of stores and malls.

Kant had already thought of this, noting that "man, because of the freedom he has in his causality, seems to consider all natu-ral things beneficial: many of them for foolish aims (such as col-orful bird feathers to adorn his clothes or colored earths or plant juices for make-up), but others for reasonable aims, such as hors-es for riding, oxen and—in Minorca—even donkeys and pigs for plowing" (CJ 246). I have yet to see a pig plowing along the streets of Whampoa or Sheung Wan, but there is a wealth of make-up and styles that lure the eyes toward beauty.

All this talk of "World Cities" is not new, although it now takes on the different inflections of global media and capital. Already in the 19th Century, Berlin was talked of as a *Weltstadt* and certainly others have fit into that category of being the center of an in-creased density of worldwide connections, wealth, and creative productivity. At this point in history, all the major cities are be-coming capitalist world cities. They are not metropoles in the old colonialist sense, standing at the center of relatively well-estab-lished empires, but they do exert a similar magnetism for finance, jobs, and innovation, as they become multilayered nodes in the network of globalized traffic.

Like all the world cities, Hong Kong is under constant de- and con-struction. It's always (un)building itself, both vertically and

84

horizontally, though there are more limits for the latter, given the geography. Tunnels, subways, skyscrapers, expansion into the green zones, and land reclamation. It's all here, all close at hand. An experiment in social and physical design, Hong Kong is a series of reflecting surfaces, a series of linguistic improvisations in Cantonese, Putonghua, English, French, German, Tagalog, Hindi, Punjabi, Arabic, Malay, Italian, and a concatenation of dialects about which I am completely ignorant. In this hum of languages, we are no longer in the historical space of the classical European male *flâneur* idling in front of the huge glass show-windows of the new *grands magasins* of an earlier century, but, instead, are always caught in the grit of the crisscrossed lines of power, are always travelling along digitized webs—though not without obstacles and surveillance from all over the world and from far above the earth—as we stroll about Hong Kong with our handhelds.

Kennedy Town, named for a British governor of the colony and not the American president, is a place worth watching exactly along these lines. When next I'm in Hong Kong, there will be new luxury high rises, new student dormitories, new eateries, new MTR stations. We'll see how Cooper's, the incense and grave-goods sellers, Mr. Ho's Pleasant Massage, the sidewalk altars, and the hole-in-the-wall noodle shops are doing. I'm hoping they'll find a way to survive, thrive, in the shadows of world finance, but it will be difficult. Laundry will still need to be done, but if things move in the predictable way, it will soon be done by a global chain of Laundromats.

§

The Lebanese Café on Lyndhurst Terrace. Before wandering back down to the Man Mo Temple, I dip into the café where there are the haunting strings of Middle Eastern music, old photographs of Lebanon (whether they are "authentic" I have no idea), a rather garish color-scheme on the walls, and a tacky painting of a wealthy woman wrapped in colorful satin robes. A bit of tame orientalism in the midst of Hong Kong. Red, green, and clear glass form the little lamp shades. The lunch of hummus, sujuk, pita, and Coke is excellent, filling. Everywhere in the world are Lebanese restaurants, food being the easiest port of entry for all the diasporas spreading around the globe along flight paths and freight paths.

I pay the bill, then wander around the corner and take the short hike down Hollywood. The Temple is next to Ladder Street— a steep cliff of stairs that leads from one level of the city to the next—and just up from Shun Tak on the harbor. It's quiet so far, Sunday morning on a Friday afternoon, with soft light suffusing the city. The Temple is an essential part of this repose. Places like the Man Mo exude a kind of serenity, even in the midst of the megalopolis. Money changes hands—from human to human and from human to the gods—constantly, but it is not, not exactly, "business" in the same manner as across the street or down the road since a narrowly defined "profit" is not the goal of the exchange. As everywhere, there is a wish for prosperity, virtue, and happiness, a better life all around, and there are gifts given toward that end. Here, with every exchange, there is also an act of gratitude, a "thank-you" travels with every joss stick, bow, or exchange of coins. The ancestors are close by, waiting for us to join them.

Man Mo is smack in the middle of high-rise Hong Kong, but an older city, an older opening toward the earth, is also preserved here, held in reserve. A steady stream of visitors, locals and tourists, move in and out of the Temple, lighting incense and purchasing Hell Money to toss into the burning oven just outside the doors, which, like the Ming Tombs outside Beijing, are marked with a high threshold. Ghosts, thank goodness, can't jump. Inside, it's full of fragrant smoke of all the coils and sticks of burning incense. Perhaps the gods thrive on the number of offerings and the thickness of the smoke?

Young and old, male and female are lighting the sticks and bowing to the many gods, with Man and Mo at the center of the action. Stepping outside and around the corner from the main altar is a smaller enclave with an altar and a room full of boxes with texts and photographs—perhaps they hold the ashes of the ancestors?—a fortune-teller, who can see the future in English, and a souvenir shop. I buy a small statuette of Kwan Yin, Goddess of Mercy, and nod in the direction of the fortune-teller. Maybe next time.

The exterior decorations are still vivid, though much of the roofline has been charred or removed. There are discontinuities along the architectural line of transmission, and apparently it's not the type of thing to renovate with new replacement materials. There is something appealing about this lack of upkeep—the brokenness of history that nonetheless supports an active relationship between the living, the dead, the gods, and the city. The world is red-hot incense and its ash drifting in invisible clouds across the harbor.

At the university, the class is deep into the snarled language of the *Critique of Pure Reason*. It is a superb group of students, gathered from Hong Kong, the mainland, the U.S., and the Netherlands. They are vivaciously thoughtful and full of the love of philosophy (except, perhaps, for two of them, whom I nonetheless find wonderfully amusing, since for some reason they prefer the guitar to Kant). We are talking about the everydayness of experience and how Kant tries to make sense of its possibility with his transcendental idealism. He is not, of course, satisfied with a description of the empirical world, regardless of how sophisticated that might be mathematically, scientifically, or socially. Hume is the angelic devil always standing on his shoulder, chuckling with good-humor at all the fervid intellectual machinations of German idealism. Kant is in the corner, sweating, wishing that the air-conditioner propped in the window actually worked. His head is swimming a bit as we talk about the *Critique*. It sounds strange to him, unfamiliar. How was he able to write that book? What does it mean?

The empirical world—sitting in a classroom with an old computer, a dusty chalkboard, rickety wooden chairs—is wild with contingencies. Kant recognizes this profound peculiarity, but he also recognizes another: *the world is ordered*. The world occurs, for us, as an arrangement of determinations, predications that are arranged as knowable successions of both time and space. While the world is not absolutely predictable it does provide the grounds for reliable and predictable knowledge. This world can never be unfolded out of pure conceptuality, but only out of the sensibility of intuitions that are given to our capacity for receptivity. We open our eyes in the morning and there is the world. We close our eyes at night and the world keeps worlding. Kant is not a radical subjectivist idealist who believes each of us concocts the world out of our own transcendental ego. This begins, however, to get at Kant's conundrum and why his work provides such an impetus for the next generation of Romantics. There is new knowledge produced all the time and there can be no knowledge, no experience at all, without a congruent structure of mind-world already in place that acts as a kind of launching platform for the extension of our knowledge.

This is why he works with such assiduity to develop the concept of the synthetic a priori, for this (and only this) structure gives him both aspects of what his system requires: a regulatory architectonic for generating the new. Experience is different than knowledge, which is produced under the laws of the understanding that will give Kant a means from distinguishing knowledge and illusion, truth and falsehood, sense and non-sense. Distinctions within distinctions within distinctions. Nothing without difference that is then rebuilt, synthesized into similarities. Kant pursues analytic work at its most profound as he establishes the grounds for synthesis.

To accomplish this task, Kant undertakes a method of twofold interpretation. Every object of experience can be unfolded both toward the empirical description of its existence *and* toward the transcendental conditions necessary for the possibility of its existence. "We assert, then," Kant writes, "the empirical reality of space, as regards all possible outer experience, and yet at the same time we assert its transcendental ideality—in other words, that it is nothing at all, immediately we withdraw the above condition, namely, its limitation to possible experience, and so look upon it as something that underlies things in themselves" (CPR 72). Space is *both* real and ideal: real for the understanding with its sensible intuitions and ideal for reason with its necessity to think the thing-in-itself. Time, too, is both empirical and transcendental. Space and time, but only as a priori aesthetic forms, give us the possibility of the empirical sense of all experience. The outside gives the inside of experience, but we can only think about, never experience, that outside.

Kant, then, advocates the double-vision of empirical investigation—whether of the particular sciences or simply the observation of the streets of Hong Kong—and of transcendental reflection. The latter has a certain priority for the task of philosophy, for it is philosophy's task to undertake the labor of thinking about itself as the necessary ways in which thinking encounters, and shapes, the otherness of the *ding-an-sich* or of the world as a whole. The sense that thinking cannot think without always othering itself, in fact, is among the principle reasons why twentieth century philosophy focuses so insistently on difference and on the other as a (non)category of thought.

The rain has started cascading down in great heavy sheets, its rumbling arrival announced by the crack of thunder rolling in from the South China Sea. The air is cooler, refreshed, as the rain cleanses the streets of Kennedy Town, North Point, Causeway Bay, and Tsim Tsa Tsui. The water streams down the slick glass walls of the highrise banks and the luxury flats, washes the grime from the H-shaped public housing blocks and the enormous glass sheaths of the shopping malls, causes the spring flowers of the future to bend their petals outward in jubilant exaltation, and washes away the effluvia of the harbors. The water from the skies opens another aspect of life that glistens ahead of us, beckoning. This is not another world nor is it a utopia of the future that will become realized in the perfect friction- and death-free society fantasized by technocapitalism. It is this very world washed with a hard rain. The Maersk Line and the Yang Ming Line, the white yachts, the lumbering ferry to Lamma, and the fishing sampans all ply the waters, refreshed in their tasks.

This writing in the rain is made possible by the conjunction of the pure forms of sensibility and the pure forms of transcendental logic: the categories of quality, quantity, relationality, and modality. These, for Kant, are the universal attributes for any object of any possible experience. Empty categories until "filled"; indeterminate "mere" forms until determined by an object. This is why Kant is not a Platonist, for the world of experience of sensible intuitions is "all" that there is, but this world itself—the rain coming down hard and the thunder receding in the distance—is always and necessarily shaped by a transcendental logic and regulated by the regulative Ideas of self, God, and freedom. The "forms" are always in-folded into experience, not encountered as concepts as we ascend out of the cave of sensory illusion. (Reason, too, will have its necessary illusions and cast perhaps the darkest of shadows on the history of modernity.)

The rain slants diagonally down as it pours from the clouds, driven by a "freshening wind from the southeast," according to the Hong Kong Meteorological Society. "But though all our knowledge begins with experience, it does not follow that it arises out of experience" (41), Kant says in the famous opening to the *Critique of Pure Reason*. The rain is completely rain even though "rain" will be said differently in English, German, Putonghua, or Cantonese. The raininess of rain, which is simply the experience of rain in all of its multiple dimensionality, is *given* to us as subjects, as the ones who are able to experience rain *as* rain. The "as" opens the totality of the world of all possible meanings and depends, absolutely, on language. We receive the rain as given in what Kant calls the "manifold of pure intuition" (CPR

112). But this is not, certainly not enough, not yet at any rate, to count for Kant as "knowledge." Perhaps this is a mistake on his part and it will need to wait for all the more recent philosophers of the "tacit" and the "everyday" for its correction.

"The second factor involved is the *synthesis* of this manifold by means of the imagination" (CPR 112). There are different sense impressions—wetness, silveriness, scent—that are bound together by the productive imagination into the experience of "I am experiencing rain" or, more simply, "it is raining." (Does the "I think" accompany each moment?) It is the "concepts which give *unity* to this pure synthesis and which consist solely in the representation of this necessary synthetic unity" that also provides the "third requisite for the knowledge of an object" (CPR 112). Concepts are forms of the understanding (and it is by no means clear how Kant finally reconciles the imagination with the understanding). Nonetheless, whatever name we give to the force that binds together, we do have an experience of differences-in-unity and of unities being unbound and dispersing.

The givenness of sensibility+synthesis+conceptuality is the sequence of the formation of the object we call "rain" that can only occur "in" consciousness. This is a logical sequence through which Kant can think distinctions, but it is obviously not a chronological sequence that occurs in the order 1,2,3. Sensibility and understanding are the two "sources" of experience, but there is a simultaneity of these operations. Givenness + synthesis + conceptual unity is a dynamic matrix of transcendental-empirical force that configures all objects—which are always complex differentiations and not simple essences—in relation to a subject of experience: the *I am, I think*. The world and subjectivity, of both the transcendental and the empirical sort, are co-requisites. The linkage, or articulation, will receive various names. I write the rain; you read the rain. The rain itself is easing up as I write. What is happening?

All synthesis is subject to the categories; and, since experience "is knowledge by means of connected perceptions, the categories are conditions of the possibility of experience and are therefore valid a priori for all objects of experience" (CPR 171). We want to know the source and purpose of this transcendental structure of the possibility of the world, but we can never approach this absolute outside, since it is not, as such, available as an object of experience. It stands apart, distanced fundamentally and irrevocably, in order that we can experience rain, writing, eating, walking, and seeing the bright neon signs that mark the Western District. We can, Kant argues, *think* this otherness, but never grasp it as a form of knowledge. As always, he is vigorously working to establish a *limit* to the excessive ambition of human epistemological aspiration. We can explore the verdant, mountainous island, but we cannot ever truly take to the high seas beyond the edge of the land.

What do Man and Mo have to do with any of this? What figure do they form at the edge of the empirical, impossible to be "verified" but waiting for all comers there in the midst of the burning coils of incense?

§

The Island. Kant both extends the domain of human knowledge—we can verifiably know the empirical being of the cosmos—and radically delimits our knowledge: we cannot go beyond the boundaries of our finite rational condition. There is an enormous tension generated in his work that will be arduously re-thought in the 19th and 20th centuries. "We have now," he concludes, "not merely explored the territory of pure understanding, and carefully surveyed every part of it, but have also measured its extent, and assigned to everything in its rightful place" (CPR 257). This is a staggeringly audacious claim from the Mapmaker of the Absolute and Its Limits (and in this moment the kin of Robinson Crusoe on his island domain). But that title will eventually go to Hegel, for Kant continues his musings on philosophical cartography by demarcating the region he has explored and setting it "inside" a more encompassing, if that's the word, mystery of the ocean.

> This domain is an island, enclosed by nature itself within unalterable limits. It is the land of truth—enchanting name!—surrounded by a wide and stormy ocean, the native home of illusion, where many a fog bank and many a swiftly melting iceberg give the deceptive appearance of farther shores, deluding the adventurous seafarer ever anew with empty hopes, and engaging him in enterprises which he can never abandon and yet is unable to carry to completion. (CPR 257)

Nature, the ultimate boundary-giver, has decreed that the knowable land of truth is a small enchanted island surrounded by the storms of illusion. Prospero, Caliban, and the lovely Miranda are singing close by, as if they had learned the ancient song of the sirens and then entered stealthily into the *Critique*. Odysseos, in disguise, is singing his own tale and Penelope is weaving and unweaving as she waits on Ithaka.

In fact, Kant is held in thrall to the island, to the sea, and to the strand in between the two, for, in order to become a mapmaker he must become familiar with all three domains even if he is torn between the temptation of the explorer and the technical requirements of the cartographer. Just out of reach, but surely reachable, is another shore. Surely paradise awaits if we but journey onward, take just one more step, or even less than a step—perhaps a step backward or to the far side of the island?—along the path of knowledge.

Kant is profoundly torn, pulled with irresistible force in opposing directions, and, already, before it has barely begun, the dialectic that is stuttering into motion is brought to a stand-still. This is a task that neither Kant nor the rest of us can ever abandon and yet it is also one that we can never complete.

The machinery of thinking does not mesh and the gears grind jaggedly together. The architectonic of philosophy is already crumbling (but the *Critique of Judgment* also waits for Kant to arrive at the need, if not quite the capacity—for no one has ever possessed that—that will require him to attempt to write a book on art, nature, teleology without teleology, the as-if, and reflective judgment that determines nothing). Nonetheless, Kant decides to take to the uncharitable and unchartable waters and leave the land of assurance, with its tempting enchantments, in his wake. But before he heads out toward the encounter the monsters, or whatever may be there beside the shifting mirages that can never fulfill epistemological desire, he recommends that we look one last time at the map of the land that he has so assiduously constructed with words.

"Before we venture on this sea, to explore it in all directions and to obtain assurance whether there be any ground of such hopes, it will be well to begin by casting a glance upon the map of the land which we are about to leave..." (CPR 257). As we head out, we must one more time turn around and see where we have been, even though there is no reason to assume that the sea and the land are isomorphic or even analogous. The old map, however complete it may be, will perhaps be of no use as we set out into the depths. We must, he insists, ask first "whether we cannot in any case be satisfied with what it contains—we are not, indeed, under compulsion to be satisfied, inasmuch as there may be no other territory upon which we can settle..."(CPR 257). There may be nothing else out there, not the slightest piece of flotsam or jetsam, no old planks of the ship to serve as a raft out there in the wide waters of the white whale. Ishmael will never have the chance to command us to call him by name. We *must*, therefore, be sure we have constructed the map of this small island and one that perhaps gets smaller all the time until it vanishes in muons, quarks, and the Higgs-boson that uphold and collapse the cosmos from the inside out.

This is the very panic of philosophy. Maybe, after all, we were wrong. Maybe, after all, we missed something, a logical connector perhaps? An observation or a correct syntactical relationship? Maybe the map is not to the correct scale or our measurements are just a hair off, which will skew the results forever, creating great waves of errancy that sweep in a philosophical tsunami across the whole of the whole. Maybe, after all, there is a small tear, a rip in the paper that annihilates the very point marked by truth?

Secondly, we have to re-examine where we have been, and how we have represented it, and ask "by what title we possess even this domain and can consider ourselves as secured against all opposing claims" (CPR 257). If map-making, with its sketches, drafts, measurements, and the necessity of empirical representation might be on the verge of failure, we then turn to legislative and legal discourse and ask what gives us "title" and "security" against all claims. Since we are our own law-givers, only the adequacy of our investigation will insure us against other claims to our island. Pirates abound, scurvy buccaneers with their rusty cutlasses and black eye-patches who invade the balmy shores as if from nowhere. So Kant will, once again and in a more compressed form, show us how he has established a secure zone.

This is the necessity of philosophy: to always be beginning again. As we move ahead, as we prepare to step off-shore and push our frail craft through the first line of breakers: let's review where we've been, let's re-examine everything from the ground up. This is the double-movement of philosophy and the arts, and one that the sciences, bless their hearts, feel that they must forego, having no need of history. So Kant begins again: "We have seen that everything which the understanding derives from itself...." (CPR 258). Kant the Mapmaker, the Legislator, and the Explorer par Excellence, will not leave us in the lurch. He will insure that he has passed the map of the island along to us with the right dimensions and a clearly readable key. This is why we must make the distinction between the phenomenal world of appearances and the noumenal thing-in-itself.

> The concept of the noumenon is thus a merely *limiting concept*, the function of which is to curb the pretensions of sensibility; and it is therefore only of negative employment. At the same time it is no arbitrary invention; it is bound up with the limitation of sensibility, though it cannot affirm anything positive beyond the field of sensibility. (CPR 272)

Is it still raining outside or has the sun broken through the clouds over Lamma Island? I'll slide open the balcony door and take a look, fill the form of the question with a determinate sensible intuition. The smudge of the island is visible, but just barely, through the bright haze.

§

Chinese New Year is just around the corner and the city is in full preparation mode. A week of celebration as the moon makes its yearly trek across the sky, as the red and gold banners are appearing in shop windows and over the entrances to flats and the parades are forming in the back-rooms, preparing to make their gaudy entrance onto the stage of the city. Luck and prosperity. The paper offerings and ghost money sellers are doing a brisk business as Hong Kongers prepare to honor the gods, the ancestors, their families, and their hopes for increased wealth in the New Year. The well-off are making travel plans to leave the teeming city behind and head for the beaches of Thailand or Bali. The moon waxes and wanes in its journey across the sky, but the hope, for us humans, is of an ever-increasing abundance.

For Kant, this is a question of history and the "perpetual peace" that enlightenment might bring with it. He sees very clearly the "folly, childish vanity...[and] the idiotic course" (UH 12) of human history, but he still wants to discover a "clue" to the progress of history on the scale not of the individual—we're all fools and babbling idiots—but on the level of the species itself. If there is no teleology, then "we no longer have a lawful but an aimless course of nature and blind chance takes the place of the guiding thread of reason" and human beings become only a "contemptible plaything" (UH 13). Kant, however, is no nihilist and with the gifts of freedom and reason to support us he hopes we can create a "second nature" of a culture that will support individual, political (with a cosmopolitan constitution), and species

transfiguration. It is up to us, in an arduous process of enlightenment, to bring the scattered seeds of historical wisdom that that
nature has planted in us to fruition so that progress can be made
on the face of the earth. (Kant admits that it might different for
those from other worlds, for whom, perhaps, even their individual destinies might come to fulfillment.)

For now, as the New Year approaches, I'll buy hell money—this
would throw Kant into a conceptual rage—and incense sticks
from the little open-air shop in Hau Wo street that sits next to Mr.
Ho's Pleasant Reflexology. Although I will pass on the "basic set"
of daily accoutrements of clothes to TVs, computers, and cars
that make up the traditional gift to the dead—after all, they, too,
need the finer things of life and the life of the dead must resem-
ble the life of the living—I will go to one of Tin Hau's abodes to
make my own, more metaphorical, offerings.

The large, teeming Temple at Wong Tai Sin has recently implanted electronic chips into fifty sets of bamboo sticks used for
fortune telling, which will insure that devotees have the complete set to choose from. One must insure the whole by an accurate accounting and technology that can track everything, send-
ing its GPS systems even toward the horizon of the other world.
(Perhaps an RFID implanted into the skin of the corpse will assist
in this project?) Fortune-telling is a big business, since so many
people want to know what's coming, and especially in love and
money that it will be getting better. And if, as Kant argues, the
time-series of unfolding moments all occurs within the "same"
world, then it makes sense that the future is already readable,
since it must be simply another time for that which is already
present but merely invisible to the generally untrained eye of the
moment. If, on the other hand, the future is radically unknow-

able, since it will not come out of the predictable trajectories of the present, then the fortune-tellers will have a tough time of it.

Kant is walking up and down Nathan Street with his usual punctuality. He needs such a routine, whether in Königsberg or Hong Kong, in order to break the routine of his writing—in order to move the legs instead of the pen—but also for at least two additional reasons. First, because the simplest walk is miraculous as the world worlds in all of its simple complexity as he takes his afternoon stroll through the clear air of the Prussian flatlands or through the damp humidity of the subtropics. One cannot know what these are like, of course, except by sensibility, so one must get out of one's chair, stretch, use the facilities, open the door, and begin to walk. There will always be new knowledge and a new formation of the aesthetic. Philosophy, for Kant, is the articulation of the conditions of possibility that are necessary for this miracle to occur.

This is related to the second necessity for the famous Kantian stroll: as he invents a vocabulary, as he writes line after line after line and works with immense intellectual energy to understand the line, how it is drawn and how it opens up to the new, he needs to go outside and think about the boundaries that insinuate themselves between the outer and inner worlds of sense; between thinking, willing, and knowing; and between his cool, dim study and the cacophony of Kowloon in the late afternoon, the streets teeming with sweating bodies and the scent of cooking and diesel fumes mingling in the clammy air.

§

Sha Tin. Up here in the New Territories, the air is hazy, the palm fronds lazily dusted by a light breeze and the ridge of the mountains as sharp as the adamantine teeth of the dragon. This is another culture-zone from Seattle, one in which a different imaginary shapes the world, but all such zones are porous, learnable to a modest extent, translatable. Globalization connects Hong Kong with the Pacific Northwest in strikingly new ways, but there have been connections since as long as the two cities have existed. There is, for our experience, no world-in-itself; everything is always marked, re-marked, perspectival. "Here I am now" always has a content of sensible, and therefore different, intuitions. These hold whether on one side or the other of the Pacific Rim. The morning sun is rising higher in the sky; the temperature is rising along with it.

There can, finally, be no Great Wall of either stone or cybersecurity, since all cultures operate along multiple axes of similarities and differences entailed by habit, perception, signification, language, and time-space. Any attempt to build such a wall—and there are always such attempts by those in power—is doomed, eventually, to violence and failure. All cultural imaginaries consist of historical accretions, sedimentations, sublimations and displacements, excrescences, secret alleyways, and stairs that bear the imprint of millions. Bloodstains, kelp, splinters of black meteorites, broken jawbones, barnacles, medallions rubbed smooth by many hands.

The so-called natural world swirls incessantly through the so-called cultural world. Claims are made that one is separable from the other, but, for Kant, both are simultaneously co-constructed by the passive-active mind of transcendental philosophy. Each micrological shift, and they occur at a scale too small to notice, changes our identities, individually and collectively, and yet we are still able, quite legitimately, to talk about "our" and "identity." Things and selves persist through time; to persist through time is the necessary condition for all experience, including that of "our" and "identity." And, yet, such things—Kant calls them all "objects"—also become re-configured, vanish from the world altogether. I am an apparitional vanishing. There is evolution; there is annihilation. There is memory, sedimentation, anticipation. There is the telling of a fortune. I am an enzyme, a catalyst, a swarm, a biome, an abecedarian, a troubadour of the streets.

From Sha Tin, I take the MTR back to the large Temple on Wong Tai Sin Square. It is packed with New Year picnickers—the gods, too, enjoy a tasty meal—and pilgrims. There is a lovely entrance arch as one climbs a short flight of stairs after emerging from the MTR, across from a highway and the usual imposing façade of high rise apartments backed by a mountain swathed in clouds. Rows of coaches have lined up to bring in the worshippers from the city and the New Territories and crowd control barricades keep the lines moving in the right direction. Wong Tai Sin is the Great Immortal Wong, a Taoist god—once a mere mortal—who can grant healing and good favor, peace and prosperity.

Worship articles are for sale and fantastic ornate golden dragons guard the entrance at the base of the arch. As always, the incense smoke floats everywhere, suffusing the air with the scent of devotion. The devotees burn their set of paper houses offered to the ancestors in the purifying fires, then, clasping their hands in prayer, hold sticks of incense aloft, lightly touching the forehead, as they beseech the gods for favor. There are two altars of flame, one for ghost money and the other for the paper houses, furniture, and cars, but both are portals through which the gifts for the dead can pass.

The temple boasts an ochre roof topped by a pair of winged phoenixes; sticks of bamboo for the casting fortunes; and food offerings of oranges, ducks, and chickens. The fires burn hotly, their ashes redistributed by attendants to make room for the next offering. Dust to dust as everything mingles in the smoke, with hundreds of red whirligigs spinning in the whispering air. Down the stairs past the WC is the Hall of Soothsayers where rows of fortune-tellers wait for the curious, the desperate, and the faithful. The world is a whole, so any part of the world—an arrangement of bamboo sticks, for instance—should be able to cast light on the whole. Metonymical interpretation has always been a necessary art for priesthoods around the world: entrails, letters, numbers, tea-leaves, stars, texts, clouds, bamboo sticks. For Kant, this moves too closely to intellectual intuition and to the non-logic of the religious enthusiasts. After all, for him all human thinking is discursive and can take on only one thing at a time, spread out in sentences that link one next to the other and point toward the beauty of infinity.

§

Thai Massage. Central is humming. The banks and luxury goods stores have replaced the Temples and the store called G.O.D. (Goods of Desire) ironically positions itself in the position of Wong Tai Sin as the one who brings happiness. Let's buy our way into heaven. Globalization creates Central, with its quiche, brioches, hamburgers, falafel, coffee, goose, and dim sum. Pike's Place Market, the Boul Mich, and Covent Garden are all connected by the distribution systems of air, sea, and the space of ideas to the bustle around this district. Kant is a bit fidgety both in front of HSBC and at Wong Tai Sin, since the latter is as far as possible from "religion by reason alone" and its practitioners, with their incense and bamboo sticks, think "god" is an object of empirical encounter rather than the non-experienceability of an Idea, and as for the former, the arch-capitalism of shopping on Queen's Way cannot approach achieving the desireless principles of the categorical imperative or the autonomy of the will exhibiting its own freedom. Money can't buy either happiness or virtue. Fortune-telling and shopping, two forms of the same activity, would be for him simple forms of idolatry based on a profound misunderstanding of the structure of the world and of the human mind.

Gods with their outlandish costumes, crowns, painted visages, and mythological beasts that guard the inner sanctums of the local temples. Raised in a Pietist culture in which the images of the divine were all evacuated of meaning and abstracted toward the invisible, the infinite, and the indeterminate—since any determinate object, though knowable, is bound by the finitude—Kant would cringe at all of this phantasmagoria. But only certain philosophers and mystics of a certain type can breathe his thin, deracinated air and I am not sure that the lack of oxygen to the brain that occurs at such heights doesn't create permanent impairments. Most love the scent of incense, the burning tip of the joss sticks placed reverently on the forehead, the ferocious dragons, the pitted rinds of the oranges, the exchange of money with the dead, and the press of fellow travelers as they make their way around the temples and back into the streets, the high-rises. Flesh to flesh; ashes to ashes.

The forces of nature and the forces of culture are one, if differentiated. The phoenix is as real as the mangy dog, though differently, and both this world and the next depend on the exchanges of commercial interests. Why not pay off one's debts now? Forgive our debtors? Might it be possible to live life without the burden of debt of any sort—whether finite or infinite—and with a simple gratefulness that only knows "yes, yes"? Kant establishes the a priori forms of aesthetics and logic that are necessary and universal for any and all experience, but most of us care more for experience than for the explication of the conditions of experience that enable the synthesis of the manifold of apperception.

Philosophers are, as Kant might say, *peculiar*. Travelers and flâneurs are peculiar as well, for they are those that must be on the move, that must leave their armchairs or the places of their birth, the familiar homestead, and see the world from different angles, see it anew by walking, riding, flying, swimming. Kant, after all, required his walks, not simply for the fresh air, though there is always that, but so he could practice seeing, feeling, and thinking at a different pace, with different lines of sight. This is another necessary, if not *a priori*, practice of the critical philosophy. Keep on the move; keep walking. Look afresh.

Or go get a massage. I have now experienced Thai massage in Central and lived, if just barely, to tell about it. In order to be filled with Happiness and Double Prosperity, I thought I would add this to my workouts at Stanley Ho sports center and my peregrinations through the streets of the city. Over on Hollywood Rd is the Siam Massage Center managed by the talented and cruel Uraiwan. Opulent burgundy curtains hang from the walls and ornate rugs cover the floor; golden statues of the Buddha grace the nooks and crannies and a number of massage tables, replete with pillows and blankets, are lined around the room. Stepping inside, one steps worlds away from the light, heat, and hectic jostling outside the door just across from the old Police Headquarters. Coming toward me with a warm greeting, Uraiwan smiled, as if she knew something I didn't, and beckoned me over to one of the curtained chambers, handing me a black T-shirt and loose wrap-around pants to change into.

In my new costume, I lay on the table and Uraiwan, still smiling, entered the curtained chamber and started kneading my back. I was tight, but it all began simply enough with her fingers finding every knotted strand of muscle and compressed fascia along my shoulders and down my spine. And then the tone began to change. Uraiwan, a smart and attractive woman on the outside, suddenly showed her cruelty as she became all knuckles, knees, and elbows. Every sharp surface of her body knifed into my back, piercing muscle and nerves I had never suspected the existence of. She climbed on my back on all fours, her knees and elbows slowly and painfully working their way down into the core inflexibilities of tissue. I wanted to scream, or counterattack, but I thought that, for a Thai, that might be seen as impolite. I exhaled, and exhaled again. The pain receded for a moment, but then Uraiwan stood up on my back and started walking along my spine. I shouted to Man, Mo, and Wong Sin Tai to preserve me, but Uraiwan showed no mercy, digging her toes in as if she were navigating a treacherous goat-path in the mountains. She climbed down and I breathed a huge sigh of relief, thinking that we were done, I could thank her and pay the fee, and then go find a large mocha latte to help me recover.

No such luck. She had me sit on my knees while she placed her own knees against my lower back and stretched me toward her, twisting this way and that, as if I were being broken on the rack. She wanted my spine to crack, but I was resisting too much, until, finally, I heard the sharp break and she chuckled, victorious. She gently released me, lay the blanket on top of me, and pounded the length of my body with tiny explosive karate chops. "Finished," she said, and I started weeping with relief, knowing I would live for another day. I changed out of my costume and back into street clothes, paid the HK178 fee, and thanked her with a small bow and the slightly hysterical smile of someone who had survived a near-death experience.

Then I stepped out of the cool darkness and back into the commotion of Hollywood. I had survived the ancient ritual of the Elbows of Uraiwan and knew, again, that the body opens itself to the world in ways we cannot imagine, since we all develop defensive habits to hold ourselves for as long as we can to the surface of the earth. We habituate ourselves to our own posture and kinesphere. The world is the body of the Buddha, but the Buddha, unlike us, is absolutely practiced in the absolute opening of the body-world. I turned right out of Siam Massage and passed on the mocha latte, instead heading for the Kosmos Café for a strawberry and banana smoothie that they called the Bliss.

One cannot imagine Kant visiting Uraiwan's studio for a Thai massage—not unless he could first prove to her that it fit the criteria for the categorical imperative or gave access to an experience of the sublime—but he certainly does not stand against the body, either of human beings or of the natural world as a whole. And, in discussing the intellectual nature of his understanding of the sublime, Kant notes that the "agreeable lassitude we feel after being stirred up by the play of affects is our enjoyment of the well-being that results from the establishment of the equilibrium of our various vital forces. This enjoyment comes to more in the end than what Oriental voluptuaries find so appealing when they have their bodies thoroughly kneaded, as it were, and have all their muscles and joints gently squeezed and bent..." (CJ 134). Uraiwan might have been able to teach him a thing or two and certainly would not describe herself as a "voluptuary."

There is, for Kant, only one world, but this world is strangely folded, divided into multiple functions. All experience is *of, to,* and *for* a rational consciousness—otherwise we would not even raise such questions—but there is no rational consciousness without sensibility. This is simply the type of creatures that we *are,* and, as such, there are no intellectual insights by which we can know God, freedom, the soul, or the numinosity of the world in and of itself. It is always oriented toward us and our (lack of) capacities. The world is an infinity of differentiations, but the gathering mediations of the categories—the necessary predicates of all possible objects—and the schematism that binds together sensibility and understanding through the productive imagination allow us to know the natural world in very precise ways (physics and chemistry actually work), to think the regulative ideas, and to undertake those peculiar activities of philosophy and travel.

The regulative ideas of God, freedom, and the soul are not objects of knowledge, since, although predicates can be connected to these terms as subjects, they cannot ever be "found" in the sensible world. (They exhibit sentential sense, but not reference.) "Please, go measure the extent of God or freedom and bring me an example of each so that we might dissect them into their constituent parts." We do not argue over the correct weight of a parakeet or a rhinoceros: we weigh them. We do not argue over the length of a piece of string or the distance between the earth and the sun: we measure them. Weight and measure, however, do not show themselves immediately to our perceiving consciousness, but must be calculated, determined through systematic methods of instrumentation made possible by our rationality, even though no one knows *why* this is the case.

Kant is always extremely cautious about the claims of reason and such evidence does not lead to a conclusion that we know the *ding-an-sich*, God, or even the "I." He will always, with great modesty, distinguish between the lack of the knowledge of the transcendent—for that is the bad old dogmatic metaphysics— with the necessity of the transcendental, which provides the conditions for the possibility of experience. A priori means a priori. Such Kantian regulative ideas exist as the uncrossable exteriority of knowledge, an absolute outside that can never come "into" the domain of the humanly knowable. But the absolute outside gives itself to human thought, to a being-thought. It gives itself to the rationality of reason, to the moral sense, and to the judgments of taste that flicker around the beautiful

Kant also calls this inscrutability the "unconditioned." Nothing, of course, can happen to or within the unconditioned, since for anything to "happen" there must be space and time determined by the categories. That is, there must be conditions at work limiting the "un-" of the conditionless. And, yet, the thought of the unhappeningness of the unconditioned can only occur from within the domain of the happening, the finitude of space and time, which is our very conditioned condition. The entirety of the world of nature is conditioned by an unbroken and ceaseless causality—one thing leads to another, both backwards and forwards—and this infinite network cannot be traced to a moment of origin from outside the system. (Spinoza is chuckling close by.)

Kant works on these problems in the sections on physical and moral teleology in the *Critique of Judgment* as he considers whether we can know the "final cause" of the world and our place in it. What's it all about? What are we here for? How much can we know? For what should we hope? The physical world can never give us evidence of an originary "author of the world," while the moral exercise of practical reason can only give us a "subjective" reading of the need of reason to posit an originary force that grants freedom, but that can, as usual, not give us any knowledge about positive characteristics of this point of origin. Like the noumenon, the outside of the unconditioned is a pure limit, a boundary of the negative.

Nothing happens, there in the unconditioned. There is absolute and unimaginable stillness. And, yet, this silent motionlessness enables all movement. Or so we might say, but as we say it the sentences and sounds unfurl in time. These are ancient dilemmas, addressed in different ways in different traditions, but Kant, as much as he drives toward leaving the island of knowledge behind and perhaps longs for the tumultuously unpredictable seaways of freedom, intellectual intuitions, or an unbounded experience of the sublime that unbinds experience, remains consistent. The absolute law of rational creatures forbids an unmediated experience of the absolute. The law itself is off-limits, the origin is legislated as inaccessible, and all human experience remains conditioned by the conditions of all possible experience. Every single one of them, without remainder.

The island, green in the sun, is rustling with rumors, fragrant with the flora of the tropics. Hidden birds trill and the sound of the waves matches the rhythms of the heart. There is song, as if a magical enchantment, on the edge of hearing.

Kant, his head cocked, is strolling along the beach with his heavy black shoes and his walking stick.

Braemer Hill. A strong wind is blowing up the sides of the hill as I stand at the end of Wai Tsui Crescent looking toward the harbor and the Convention Center and, just beyond, the skyline of Central. I'm right in the center of Hong Kong Island and the IFC and the ICC, two majestic pillars of glass and steel that stand as monuments to capital, perfectly frame the view toward the South China Sea. The harbor, as usual, is replete with anchored vessels and ships moving in and out, ferries headed to Macau, Zhuhai, and Shantou. Fast-moving gray clouds are obscuring the Peak and all the sweat and anxiety of Central, Wan Chai, and Kowloon are invisible except for the beautiful symmetry of the skybreaker architectural forms of finance. Up here on the terrace, just down the road from Shue Yan University, one of the private schools in Hong Kong, there is an old rose-colored highrise apartment building with the drying laundry and rusting AC units, the opened cantilever windows, and the peeling corrosion of the exterior pipes.

The foliage is lush and green, full of the scents of flowers whose names I don't know with bare outcroppings of stone as the hill shears off into a ravine that becomes a high-sided gully opening out to the city and the sea below. I can imagine the rush of water during the rains, but, today, the hidden birds are singing to one another, a hawk soars high overhead, and two butterflies cavort in the space over the trees, brush, and flowers. Referring to William Marsden's description of Sumatra, which boasts a climate much like Hong Kong, Kant notes that these regions "extravagant in all its diversity to the point of opulence, subject to no constraint from artificial rules, can nourish [our] taste permanently. Even bird song, which we cannot bring under any rule of music seems to contain more freedom and hence to offer more to taste than human song, whenever this human song is performed according to all the rules of the art of music... [but] when bird song is imitated very precisely by a human being (as is sometimes done with the nightingale's warble) it strikes our ear as quite tasteless" (CJ 94). Anything that sustains itself in free play strikes us as intriguing, while the artificially ordered quickly becomes dull and boring, in need, precisely, of change and the unpredictable.

Kant must have been extremely irritated by the artificial reproduction of sound, for he returns again to the poorly imitated nightingale. "What do poets praise more highly than the nightingale's enchantingly beautiful song in a secluded thicket on a quiet summer evening by the soft light of the moon?" he asks. "And yet we have cases where some jovial innkeeper, unable to find such a songster, played a trick—received with the greatest satisfaction, initially—on the guests staying at his inn to enjoy the country air, by hiding in a bush some roguish youngster who (with a reed or rush in his mouth) knew how to copy that song in a way very similar to nature's. But as soon as one realizes that it was all deception, no one will long endure listening to this song that before he had considered so charming; and that is how it is with the song of any other bird" (CJ 169). When copying is combined with deception—and in this case the two are the same—then Kant dismisses the experience with disdain. When nature in its wildness meets the mind in its free play, however, there is intense pleasure. In the age of the simulacra, how do we determine the difference?

The birds and butterflies know how to ride the wind. It is their element, unlike with us, who have to learn the *rules* of the wind, how to complement our sluggish feet and legs (though these are related, evolutionarily, to the wings of the birds) with sails, para-gliders, parachutes, and composite wings. The hawk, its wings outstretched, is below me now, content with the wind-currents, an eye to the hunt. I love finding these outlooks, these new plac-es in which to absorb the world. The scents, the tired rose hues of the apartment tower, the city in the mid-distance. The harbor is wrinkled by the wind.

There is not much winter here, although the Hong Kongers love to don parkas, scarves, mufflers, sweaters, and ski caps as soon as the temperature drops below 55F. There is a fantasy of winter, a longing for snow, but winter has now passed and the earth is turning toward spring in this hemisphere. What are the Chinese forms of the gods and goddesses of spring? The season always produces its own local deep mythology, since we are completely dependent on the earth and its miraculous annual re-juvenation.

We are the earth whose hidden seeds are breaking through the winter ground; we are the scents floating on the wind. The flowers bloom in a quiet exaltation. We are the reclaimers of the harbor's land, the builders of skyscrapers, the digger of great tunnels. What will all of this be like in a hundred years when long ago I will have become a handful of dust thrown to the wind? I wish the man or the woman who comes to stand in this place, perhaps even with a pen or digital airwriter, all my very best. Kant, too, will be waiting for them, waiting to be read, waiting to grant the difficult gift of the task of reading the questions raised, and left behind like crumbs, on the trail of philosophy.

§

Happy Valley and Causeway Bay. A dismal and failed attempt to find the Police Museum after wandering around Causeway Bay to see the Happy Valley Racecourse. Money, style, visibility, and horses: what could be better? The track was quiet, though, when I visited, waiting for the arrival of the thundering hooves and the rustle of the local currency. For me, this was an obligatory visit, but I am not really interested in horses, so I headed up Leighton Road to Kennedy. On the map, it looked as if Kennedy intersects Wan Chai Gap Road, but either the map was erroneous or I simply missed the connection. But whenever we fall off the map, there is something else in front of us, just to the side, beneath our feet and over our heads. There are no gaps in the geography of the world. We may be lost, in more ways than one, but the world always gives us its usual coordinates. It is seamless. Since I had missed the Museum, one I had been looking forward to, I kept following Kennedy—after a break for chips and a soda at a local filling station—as it wound its way beneath large shady trees.

The Botanical Garden a delightful space of respite, falls off the slope in one direction and expensive apartment buildings line the upside of the slope. Where do all these people with all this money come from? What do they actually do all day? Gamble with money, of course, their own and other peoples'. In one way or another, they *trade*. Kennedy, losing its line at last, falls off onto Garden Rd and Lower Albert, past the AIA building and the Bank of China. It's good to come upon the power of global capitalism from the rear. I missed the Police Museum, but there is nowhere I have walked that is without the presence of the law. Like the coordinating of the world, the law, too, is seamless. It enwraps us wherever we go, however far we travel.

This is one of Kant's immense questions as he settles, dressed in his formal magistrate's robes once again, into the raised wooden chair of the High Court. The law is high, but its height reaches the lowest of the low regions of the world. It has a long arm, long legs that can be anyplace at any time, and a large white wig to indicate its pompous hilarity and artificiality. The law is ritualized convention; the law of the law is indomitable, intransigent, and unavoidable. We are legislators and legislated. How is it that the world is coherently created and maintained? How is it that rational creatures, such as ourselves, can have accurate knowledge and a place that fits us?

Empirically we are of course "from" somewhere and somewhen, but we are, and always have been, always on the move. We are nomads of the streets and the steppes. Time, that a priori god, insures that temporality, like spatiality, is seamless and keeps us moving from moment to moment, keeps each moment saturating us to the very limit and beyond, for time, sooner or later, breaks each of us apart and disperses us in death. Time is the excess of every measure even as it grants certain forms of measure (related to movement, spatiality, and therefore the "common" notion of time).

Transcendental understanding gives "reasons," "rules," "logics," and "laws" that govern our sensibility and enable us to have a world rather than an incoherent flux. That is decidedly strange. We can make sense of (at least some) things; mind is meaning imprinting the world with its signature, but the world is not-thinkable without mind always already at work. The mind-world stitches together language; language stitches the world-mind. This is the possibility necessary to allow us to create "coherent stories" about the police, triads, horse-racing, and a long hot walk down Kennedy Road. Kant remains, bewigged, in his law chambers at the High Court, pondering the legislative action of freedom and the highest of the high, the holy.

But down in Causeway Bay there are swarms of humanity walking the narrow streets. A mass of young Indonesian men and women in jeans, T-shirts, cut-offs, and backwards caps—the accoutrements of teenagers around the world—are browsing the streets for bags, shoes, music, and each other. There are many money exchanges around this area that the millions of expatriate workers from other parts of Asia use to ship funds back home to those not able, or willing, to board a plane or a boat to go make money working at menial jobs in a rich city. Cleaning, child-care, sex workers, and security guards seem to be the main tasks. The women congregate on Sunday in parks and public squares, under roadways or along the concrete hallways of indoor markets. I wish I knew the language, knew their stories.

In every center of capital, there are these tight circles of low-wage mobile workers, moving across the face of the planet seeking a financial advantage, however slight. They live in the small quarters of luxurious high-rises in the Mid-Levels or they huddle in sweltering abandoned container boxes or in the cramped flats of public housing. There is an intensity in the rhythm of the prowl through Causeway Bay restaurants and shops in the ceaselessly moving swarm of humanity. From this urban crossroads, the roads split into many directions—up toward Happy Valley and down toward the MTR station, and, just beyond, the harbor. How cool and inviting the water looks. There is constant traffic, motorized and on foot, and the pedestrians negotiate the streets in multiple forms of movement: waiting or not-waiting for the light; scurrying diagonally across the intersections; swinging shopping bags or sipping drinks and zipping back and forth from the colorful screens of their mobiles. Text and image; the possibility of love.

Jardine's Bazaar and Jardine's Crescent are nearby, typical market streets packed with clothes, toys, handbags, shoes, and souvenirs. The city is crammed with goods, piled high with stuff. There's something for everyone; indeed, more than something. I'm surprised the island doesn't sink under their weight. The piles of goods here can be touched and fondled, imagined on a shoulder or in the closet, and organized on an entirely different principle than that of the swanky display windows that stage the strange objects of desire behind thick panes of glass. The city hums along in its own incomparable rhythm, shaping all of us to its shapes, its surfaces, textures, scents, sights, and noises. It's the rich and the poor, the stylish and the destitute, as an ad for Sabina Swimwear passes by on the side of a bus.

§

Aberdeen's Marine Club. I hopped on the #59 bus over to Aberdeen and its factories, high rises, swanky yachts, and floating restaurants. Never having been here, I started walking around the area in order to orient myself. This is a working neighborhood, full of the usual nautical shops, including Adventure Ships, Wah Kee Stainless Steel Workers, and the Hop Hing Sum Kee Shipyard. Fences guard the road on both sides. It is the backside of the harbor, cluttered with boats from rusted scows to yachts; corrugated tin shops and warehouses; repair shops; junk; cast-off engines and parts; coiled cables and wires; Shing Ge Fat shipyard; Neway Shipping Ltd; Starship Yachts; Asia Service Center; wakeboarding.com.hk; Skywave; Sun Hing shipyard; Ming Kee

Marine; Master Yacht Service Center; Shui Wan Marine Svc; and the Folkland Shipyard (founded 1893). There is, in addition to the Bus Terminal, the Aberdeen Marine Police Base, Noble Brand Investments Ltd, a Park-n-Shop, and Shum Wan Pier Drive, off of which is moored the Jumbo Floating Restaurant.

What does it mean, finally, to orient oneself "in" and "to" the world and then to "set sail"? These might well be near-equivalents, since, for the most part, we know where we are going and how to get there. We plot a course, using coordinates familiar to us or to those who have come this way before us. There are nautical maps that chart every reef, every sandbar, every sunken ship, every buoy that will lead us safely through dangerous waters. There are GPS devices in our cars and in our phones. So for a very long time—and for our whole lives in a very real sense—we walk paths and sail sea-trails laid down by others. This area is brand new for me and therefore touched with a modest exhilaration, but this route has been oriented by a host of others. I move through this space as I move through my projection of space toward the horizons.

Things are not precisely repeated: the unexpected can always intervene—death, accident, and discovery are structurally always at hand—and I will always experience the event of this orientation of spacetime differently than any other. The world is "my" world; it is "our" world. This is part of the very fabric of being. There is a sweater and a pair of pants hanging out to dry. Yellow-flowering trees, a bird singing somewhere close by, but invisible. We can only travel more deeply along the surfaces into the worlding of the world. There is no other place; there can be no other place. Death is a threshold for the passage of ghosts; it is, perhaps, a door, but for us this is an absolutely opaque portal which, as much as we attempt to run our finger along it or even just to think it, always vanishes before we can make contact. We see dy-ingness and livingness; we see a dead object called a "corpse," but death itself is in-comprehensible. I am on a bench in the Shum Wan Drive Setting-Out Area. Here and now: a bird is sing-ing, a young man is strolling by with his iPod, earbuds, and Vita-Soy. I need do nothing to be oriented to the world at this level, for I am always placed in a time. In other ways, however, there is much more work to be done.

We do become more oriented the longer that we are alive, the more densely overlaid and crisscrossed is the texture of our expe-rience, and, if we are lucky, we keep our wits about us. We be-come more oriented largely by extending the repertoire of our habits, but, if we are lucky, we also become more disoriented as well as we come to recognize—though this is a vexed term in this context—the peculiarity, the foreignness, the utter strangeness of it all. Look again at a duck, a dragon-fly, a hippopotamus—just say the word, with all those plosive "p"s—a ship, a palm with its riverine lines, a cloud, a star, or a double-decker tram, festooned with advertising, rollicking slowly on its tracks down Des Voeux Road.

For Kant, such a field of orientation is based on perception, on the faculty of understanding as well as on the transcendental mediating structures of all possible experience, including the transcendental aesthetic a prioris of space and time, the catego-ries, the table of judgments, and the schemata. We are, at this level, at home in the world in the sense that our body, and the body of all possible empirical experience, mysteriously offers it-self in alignment with the mind. Not one without the other, Kant maintains. There is an attunement at work for each of us, a commensurability that gives the world form, which, for Kant, always exhibits necessity and freedom, natural causality and the moral will.

But there is also the very odd fact that newness emerges, that we can come to experience and understand the new. Kant is caught between his profound desire to explore the territory of the knowable and the philosophical vocation to think at the very limit of understanding and the desire, if possible, to peer beyond the edge, around the corner. But here there be dragons; here there be the mirages of the mind, the transcendental illusions of reason itself. Reason is a trickster. Reason sets traps, but then seems to be able to set traps for the traps it has set for itself. We, necessarily, create transcendental illusions, but, if we are careful, we can catch ourselves creating the illusions. The illusions and antinomies cannot be "solved" as logical resolutions—they are not "problems" in this sense—but we can vigilantly guard against them and not tarry longer than necessary down their primrose paths of perilous thorns.

Here in Aberdeen, the world is pure exchange. Time passes from the afternoon to the coming of the evening and families walk through the park and the playground. Busses roll past and boats of all stripes head out of the marina. Food and water come and go; we eat and excrete; we inhale and exhale. There are the islands of memory and the vast sea, always thinking via analogy, of the unknown. Friends all gather in the lobby of the Marina, a place for the wealthy, and then walk out onto the dock in the light rain to board a yacht over to Lamma Island for seafood and beer under the bleached awnings hung with the multicolored twinkle of Christmas lights. Good company, good food, and good drink by the edge of the sea. This is the singular universal which everyone should share, even though there cannot be a rule that governs such a judgment of taste. It's the generosity of affect: come, share in this good fortune that has come upon all of us.

§

Mui Wo. As the ferry backs out of its slip, the white water churning, the iconic buildings of the HSBC, Bank of China, Jardine House, and IFC all rise skyward as we begin the run over to Lantau Island and village of Mui Wo. The ferry is a blurred metaphor for the operations of linking differences into a dynamically workable system of rules, capacities, objects; it is an image for the transfer points that connect and differentiate, like the schemata that Kant explicates, the understanding, the imagination, and reason across knowledge, judgment, and the freedom of the will required for morality. The world is the interweaving of all of these, which always occur together but which are never identical. Who knows what the schemata is? No one can really say, even if we can see its necessity and its effects. There must be something like a schemata at work, though, since world, the I, and language somehow seem to work together to make sense of things. Usually, of course, some system of recognizable boundaries remains in place, since we know the difference between "pier," "harbor," "open water," and "island."

For us, as rational human beings, one concept always links to another concept as language spins itself out—"ferry" gathers "water," "boat," "movement," and many more into a constellation of meaning—so that we are always in the domain of meanings and representation, which, even though it must assume, at least for Kant, the thing-itself that underlies and underwrites the discourse of the mind, it must also recognize that the real thing cannot be non-discursively grasped in either an intellectual or a purely sensible intuition that acts apart from the understanding. There is, for us, no such thing, no such capacity. All is bound together, but not in the sense of a predetermined universe. Everything human is discursive. Freedom gives room for play between the faculties; reflective judgments become more important than determinative ones, and—Kant is, after all, a transcendental philosopher—we are all bound up with each other and every other other. There are analytic statements in which the predicate repeats the subject (though this is open to question) and synthetic a priori events that give rise to discovery and constant surprise. The predicate is not predictable from the form of the subject.

White barf bags grace the pockets in front of each seat, just in case a violent confusion between the inside and the outside of the body occurs. With the engines growling, the pilot backs us out, then turns us around into the choppy harbor full of boats. Kowloon slips by on the right as we churn out toward deeper waters. Tugs, the Star Ferry, First Ferry VI, the orange jet ferries from Macau, and a white cruise ship move past each other as Shun Tak recedes on the port side. Cranes, reminiscent of their ornithological cousins, move like lithe beasts across the decks of the anchored container ships. We are crashing through the oncoming waves and pass a large buoy with "Victoria" painted on the side, a tiny indicator of history's presence and the long, slow recession, not without its powerful after-shocks, of the British Empire.

Mui Wo, where I am headed to visit a friend, is a slow beach town. Fishing and small powerboats are moored along the Silver River and a small branch of HSBC stands at the base of the hill near the public bathroom, McDonald's, and the China Bear Bar and Café. There is the Paradise Café, the Outlet store and an active market, government offices, rows and rows of bicycles; hikers with their bandanas and Nike walking shoes; a bus terminal to Tai O; signs for monasteries; palm trees and bare rocks; and the smooth green bay. As we begin to walk around town, there is the Silvermine Beach Hotel, a small resort standing alongside the Silver River and rugged mountains, bare and windswept, that frame the compact seaside town.

People live here because it is far more affordable than the city, but still within a short ferry ride to work. Dragon Boats have been dragged onto the sand, painted with a dragon's head that boasts small tightly wound springs for eyes. One thing stands for another and we are always thinking in analogies. (Kant has a great deal to say about the "analogies of experience," which enable us to place things and events in time.) The Fook Chui Loi and Tak Chai Kee seafood restaurants beckon, but will need to wait for another day, another life. Down in the plaza are Buddhist monks in gray robes, an older woman lugging a basket, a man in a ragged cap and dirty clothes, backpackers, and spandexed bikers who have gathered for their weekend jaunt. Costumes, clothes, and class.

From Mui Wo we head over to Tong Fuk ("Pleasant Pond"), to visit our friend's lovely refurbished home. One of the ubiquitous Tin Hau Temples sits on the outcropping looking out to sea. It has a metal door, unlocked, and is well-kept, opening up to the altar and the goddess. Inside, there is incense, fruit, a script I can't read. From there, we walk up the road to another wide beach with a long concrete pier extending into the bay with its small fishing boats. In the distance, tiny figures are gathering mussels (like the potato pickers or hay stackers in Van Gogh) with the starkness of the mountain rising behind them, putting them into perspective with the sea spreading itself out in front—shrimp boats working the bay in pairs as they drag a common net through the water. Sunburned and happily tired, we pick up the 11 Bus in Tong Fuk and head for Tung Chung, one of the new cities being built on reclaimed land and the starting point for the gondola to the Big Buddha, where we catch the MTR to Hong Kong Station from where I will catch the tram and then the bus to Kennedy Town and the flat that feels like home on Sha Wan Drive.

§

Shek-O. Shek-O, the "rocky bay," is a lovely little beach enclave on the far southeastern end of Hong Kong Island. We took the MTR toward the eastern tip of Hong Kong Island, then picked up the #9 bus from Shau Kei Wan, which rolled along the cutbacks through the mountains until pulling into the low-slung beach town. Kant is wearing hiking boots and carrying a camera with him today, holding it in his hands as if it is a foreign object, which of course it is. He would not have known about this machine to capture, shape, and store light, the digitized darkroom that mimics the eye and the mind. But he is becoming acclimatized to the subtropics, and, soon, he will be wearing shorts, a blue-flowered Hawaiian shirt, and glare-free sunglasses. The Po Toi islands are set like small emeralds in the midrange just off the coast.

After a delectable lunch of friend eggplant, morning glory, and prawns, we climbed a small rocky headland up to a pagoda. Brides and bridegrooms perched on the rocks against the dramatic backdrop of sea and mountains, where BMX and mountain bikers congregate for another photo-shoot. What would Kant think of this photography and music culture, with all of its reproductions? For us, there is no real need to visit Shek O, much less to write or read about it. We have already seen it before we arrive, since it is all visible on the image production line accessible through mobile phones. The stone meets the water and there is the white froth of the waves that, over the centuries, have scooped out dark sea-caves.

Gulls float against the milky turquoise waters. Sailboats rock at anchor, while the fishing boats slowly trawl the waters in the distance and men with long fishing poles stand on a rock at the edge of the net-littered beach. The houses of the rich are nestled away on the smaller headland in the distance—the rich can buy privacy whereas the poor must find ways to live together in tiny quarters—the tight cluster of the old part of town with its shop and fish warehouses that distribute the catch to the restaurants downtown. Small flats with their multiple antennae reaching for the invisible satellites as their laundry, as in Kennedy Town or the Wan Tsui Crescent, dries in the humid wind. The tiny Tin Hau Temple watches over it all. Gods, apparently, are not constrained by the size of their dwelling. The infinite can fit into very small places. The green waves rock against the sandy cliffs as we look out to sea.

We wander back down the hill and back into the little gathering of shops for coffee, Chocolate Charlotte, and ice cream at the Shining Stone, a funky little café like those found around the world in these beach towns. "Dust in the Wind" and "Bye Bye Miss American Pie" are on the music mix as the light rain comes on as we step outside the café and wend back to the terminal for Bus #9 to take us back up the winding roads through the hills and into the bustling crowds of the city, back to the familiar haunts of Sha Wan Drive.

Things are coming to an end for us in Hong Kong and in another few weeks we will tucked away toward the rear of Air Canada 008 headed back over the vast Pacific to Vancouver, where we will pick up the little puddle jumper to Seatac. There is so much stimulus in this place, so much work to be done, so much pleasure. The water, the sky, the mountains, the streets, the people. Turning and turning. The reflections flashing in the skyscrapers, climbing up the glass with the sun, broken occasionally by the tatters of clouds. Time in Hong Kong is fraying, slipping away, an anticipatory loss in advance of the loss, grieving (as we always do) for the end that is coming, whose arrival brooks no exceptions.

Kant does not really help much with all of this, though he reminds us of our finitude, our freedom, the longing of reason for its "endless task" of completing our moral development, and the wish for beauty to be broken asunder by the excess of the sublime. He reminds us of our need for orientation, the peculiar relation between the I and the world. He thinks about the self-destructive idiocy of our species and wonders about the directionality of history, hoping for progress toward perpetual peace. He speaks of infinity, the categories and the schemata, the elevation of practical over theoretical reason as that which grounds us in the supersensible.

For there to be philosophy, for there to be understanding as I walk through the streets of Hong Kong, bedazzled by the multitudinous sounds and scents of life, there must be freedom that in its silent and unobservable way opens the possibilities of existence. But, as Kant reminds us, "how freedom is even possible and how this kind of causality has to be represented theoretically and positively is not thereby seen; that there is such a causality is only postulated by the moral law and for the sake of it. It is the same with the remaining ideas, the possibility of which no human understanding will ever fathom although no sophistry will even convince even the most common human being that they are not true concepts" (CPrR 247). Freedom intimately touches us across all of our activities. In a succinct definition, Kant asserts that "the power of freedom [is] to pass beyond any and every specified limit" (CPR 312). A constant passing beyond limits, beyond the here-and-now, the this-and-that, toward the other. A constant walking through the streets of Hong Kong toward an elsewhere.

Reading Kant teaches us to *do* philosophy, to walk the streets of philosophy, a task that we never quite understand but that we nevertheless continue to take on as an act of faith—faith in reading, writing, the senses, thinking, and walking—that, occasionally, is punctuated with a quick pirouette of joy that comes upon us as if from nowhere and lifts us up on the toes of our scuffed shoes. Walking the streets also teaches us to read philosophy in a more fruitful manner, to test its abstractions against the rhythms of the MTR or of Nathan Road. It brings philosophy back into the city, where the whole peculiar story began.

Other walkers, even though they do not yet know it, are now headed to Hong Kong, headed to Wellington Street and Lamma Island, to Kowloon Tong and the high-rises of Central, the sweat-streaked scents of Kennedy Town, the cemetery on Pok Fu Lam, and to the choppy waters of Victoria Harbor. Kant, bewigged and bemused, glances over at me. We nod at one another and give a slight wave. It is time for him to depart from this city on the edge of the world, where the land and the water meet, and return to his daily walks along the streets of Königsberg. It is time for me to head the other way. We will meet again, though, where the land and great blue sea meet one another along the bluffs and beaches of Useless Bay.

Walking Directions

Kant, Immanuel. *Critique of Pure Reason.* Trans. Norman Kemp Smith. New York: Palgrave Macmillan, 2007.

——. *Critique of Judgment.* Trans. Werner S. Pluhar. Indianapolis: Hackett Publishing Company, 1987.

——. *Critique of Practical Reason.* Trans. Mary J. Gregor. Cambridge, UK: Cambridge University Press

——. "Idea of a Universal History from a Cosmopolitan Point of View," *Kant: On History.* Ed. Lewis White Beck. Upper Saddle River NJ: Prentice Hall, 2001.

——. "What is Enlightenment?" *Kant: On History.* Ed. Lewis White Beck. Upper Saddle River NJ: Prentice Hall, 2001.

Nietzsche, Friedrich. *Twilight of the Idols: Or, How to Philosophize with a Hammer.* Trans. Duncan Large. Oxford: Oxford UP, 2009.

——. *Beyond Good and Evil: Prelude to a Philosophy of the Future.* Trans. Walter Kaufman. New York: Vintage, 1989.

www.ingramcontent.com/pod-product-compliance
Lightning Source LLC
Chambersburg PA
CBHW031857090426
42741CB00005B/541